Dear Howard,

   Here's to a bright &
thriving future!

   My Best,

     Cathie.

Praise for *Rooted in Family*

"As I read *Rooted in Family,* I kept thinking that you cannot learn these things from a book. There is no theory, no course that teaches one to be the kind of innovative leader that Caroline is. It takes courage, creativity, seeking, exploration, and willingness to use everything that life is offering to BECOME, and then to put that becoming into action. At this time, we need leaders who bring their passion, their vulnerability, and their whole selves to their work. This is a new world, needing a new type of leadership. Caroline is someone who is grounded in values AND willing to forge new pathways in response to a changing world."

Ann Bradney, Director, Radical Aliveness Institute

"This book is wonderful on so many dimensions. It offers a fresh and loving perspective from inside one of America's most iconic families. It provides an inspiring example for all family businesses of the importance of "The Business of Family." And it tells Caroline's own inspiring story— her "heroine's journey" of personal growth that led her away from and then back to the family she loves. It is also a story born out of current times, when we are all forced to slow down, breathe, and reexamine the things that matter."

Alison Davis, Managing Partner, Fifth Era

"Bringing together journeys of personal and professional discovery, *Rooted in Family* brings to life the author's story as a member of a legacy family enterprise who carves her own path as an independent businesswoman, as a seeker of inner wisdom, and a philanthropist. It is a compelling and candid account of the obstacles and opportunities that she faced along the way, marked by her courage, honest self-reflection, resilience, and wise teachings. More than a personal story, this book offers practical guidance and teaching stories that reflect Caroline's experience both as a member and advisor to family businesses. A thoughtful and satisfying read to anyone interested in the real story of how to balance personal growth and connection in a family enterprise."

Joan DiFuria & Dr. Stephen Goldbart, Co-founders, Money, Meaning & Choices Institute

"Caroline's book is an intimate, honest, unpretentious, and heart-warming illumination of beauty grows from genuine values rooted in love for family. That love ripens with the wisdom that can only come from the endless effort and hard work necessary to nurture, strengthen, and sustain family ties. Tending to grapes is a reflection of self-care. Crushing grapes becomes a metaphor for family unity, celebration, and affirmation. She wisely chooses to measure the success of business in terms of qualities and dimensions of happiness. Her ongoing and caring commitment to independence, growth, and preserving the gifts of the founding fruits, by sharing her considerable insights is a testimony to the sweetness and resilience of the Gallo family's finest crop and the purity of the Coleman family's most precious gem."

Ben Donenberg, Founder & Executive Artistic Director, The Shakespeare Center of Los Angeles (SCLA)

"Caroline gives us an intriguing and easy-to-read story, where the lessons for multi-generational families flow naturally from the compelling personal and family narrative. As she opens the door to us into each phase of her life, we can understand the influence that family has had on her, and that she has had on her family. Whether you are thinking about engaging your family for long-term unity and success, or you just like a good biographical story, this is a very worthy read."

Alan Duncan, Founder, PWN (Private Wealth Network)

"In her book *Rooted in Family*, Caroline Bailey gives us a window into the legacy of a family business through her own personal experience and those of families she has known and guided. What we learn, even through the trials and tribulations, is that especially in these difficult times, there's no place like home and your family."

Nely Galan, New York Times bestselling author, *Self-Made*

"If you are looking for inspiration in finding anchors amid all the dynamic and changing cycles of life, look no further. Caroline shares her own story of staying grounded in herself and her family, striving for unity and connectivity. A great inspirational read that spans generations."

Barbara Hurt, Fifth Generation Brown Family, Brown-Forman

"Being the heir to a great family legacy is wonderful but also challenging. Caroline's story is about coming from two entrepreneurial families and finding her own way in life. She warmly shares the stories of her two families and her development. She could have followed a conventional path but instead, she makes some radical changes in her life and work. She shares her experiences and how she takes her learning first to her family, and then to the world in her service and work. Inspiring and candid, Caroline shows how a person from a legacy family can create her own path in life."

Dennis T. Jaffe, PhD, Research Associate, Wise Counsel Research, author *Borrowed From Your Grandchildren*

"Anyone who understands what G3, G4, and G5 means will relate to this insightful and very open and honest shared life journey. While there are many family business "text" books offering best practice approaches to how one navigates between the three circles, and/or successfully transition governance over time, few books reinforce the most important aspect of all, which is the need as a family member to find our own identity, passions, and balance, and how to live our own life, not just the life of the business. For a family business to successfully evolve *over* time, it requires both the family members and the business to concurrently evolve *with* the times. Caroline's life story is a great example of how one family member's life journey came full circle and resulted in both the family business, and herself, being better for it."

Frank Mars, Fourth Generation, Mars, Incorporated

"History, heritage, education, and talent are all family treasures Caroline Coleman Bailey brings to her journey. Join in her quest to honor her treasures as she shapes a life and a career of helping others to do the same."

Carolyn Martini, Third Generation, Louis M. Martini Family

"A beautiful first-person recollection of humble beginnings, impressive success, and the important role family plays in self-actualization. Caroline caught my attention with her colorful recounts of days gone by and kept it with her messages of positivity, independence, values, and change. Throughout her fascinating story, I found myself smiling, and resonating with the importance of one's individual journey toward happiness."

Andrew D. Pitcairn, Fourth Generation, Family Council Chair & Board of Directors, Pitcairn

"Speaking about family relationships is an art, especially when talking about your own, and honoring what you have received empowers those who come after you. That role of enabling the family to thrive is what Caroline is mastering within her own family and in others that she is helping. It takes empathy and humility—you need to walk the talk. It is the journey of an independent entrepreneurial spirit, loyal to her legacy, that will help us build our own."

Olivier de Richoufftz, General Secretary, Family Enterprise Foundation

"A sensitive story of discovering purpose on the road less travelled."

Caroline Seow, FBN (Family Business Network)

"A wonderful book—heartfelt, thoughtful, and gracefully written. I was moved and inspired by Caroline's extraordinary story."

David Sutcliffe, Actor & Core Energetics Practitioner

"Rooted in Family offers insight into the fascinating personal story of Caroline Bailey. It touches on many of the unique opportunities and challenges that come with growing up in a family business, and highlights the innovative initiatives Caroline has taken to contribute to the long-term success of her own family. Caroline's own family business background, combined with her work with families all over the world, make this book an incredible resource for all business families that want to keep their families together!"

Edouard Thijssen, Fifth Generation member of the family behind the Belgian Aliaxis Group & Co-Founder & CEO, Trusted Family

"Rooted in Family is a journey navigating a unique life that comes full circle to give each person who reads it something to think about and appreciate, and enables us to STOP, reflect and deeply understand what matters. The approach to change is unique and one that highlights the cornerstone of qualities that came together in one family, driven by one person that charted a new approach to "The Business of Family."

Denise Thomas, CEO & Founder, Apple Pie Capital

"Rooted in Family immediately resonated with me as a fourth-generation winegrower and CEO of our 137-year-old family business. Caroline explores family/work/life balance and relates the hard choices encountered on her journey. It takes courage to turn the mirror around and reflect on yourself, life's lessons, and your passions, which she does. I find her story engaging and rewarding, with many nuggets that I will embrace in my life and share forward in business."

Carolyn Wente, Fourth Generation Winegrower, CEO, Wente Family Estates

"One of the most difficult chasms for a professional advisor to cross is understanding what it is like to be inside the families they serve. For family members, it is often difficult to find a unique voice of leadership and the courage to act. Through keen insight and honest storytelling about the evolution of her own family, Caroline's invaluable offering will help family members and advisors alike."

Matthew Wesley, Managing Director, Merrill Center for Family Wealth

ROOTED IN FAMILY

ROOTED IN FAMILY

Honoring The Past
While Creating
Our Future

Caroline Coleman Bailey

PUBLISHING

ROOTED IN FAMILY
Honoring The Past While Creating Our Future

First Edition
First Printing 2020

ISBN: 978-1-7321736-6-8 (paperback)
ISBN: 978-1-7321736-7-5 (hardbound)

Library of Congress Cataloging-in-Publication Data is pending.

This work was published in the United States of America in partnership with

CARTWRIGHT PUBLISHING
Visibility ● Authority ● Legacy ● Clients

Cover & Author Photos: Matthew Visser
Cover Design: Steven Novak
Interior Design: JetLaunch
Copy Editor: Kathy Oveson

To my family — past, present, and future

CONTENTS

INTRODUCTION

Just when the caterpillar thought the world was over,
it became a beautiful butterfly...

—*Proverb*

I had long desired to write a book as a complement to my professional work with families in business together. Early in 2020, I had high hopes for growing my business, publishing my book, and more, and then the world took a turn, a big turn. I soon found myself, along with the rest of us, in the midst of a global pandemic and sheltered in place.

Being thrust into a global pandemic is not a gift, although I did receive the gift of time. Throughout my life, I always felt I did not have enough time, always being on the go, always rushing. It was my inherited chaos and I fully embraced it, while secretly wishing to quiet it all down. As the saying goes, be careful what you wish for, you might just get it, and I did. Now with all the time in the world, how to make the most of it? I fully re-engaged in my book project. I cocooned myself, and to my surprise, the book that really needed to be written emerged. What I thought would be a book written for my business emerged as a book I needed to write for myself. It has been a true cathartic experience for me, one of deep reflection and growth.

INTRODUCTION

When you let things sit long enough, they eventually "tell" you what they want to be. That was certainly the case for me. I felt compelled to write my book, although I thought it would be easier if the topic remained at arms-length. I spent many years being the spokesperson for my family business and it was always easier to speak about our history, heritage, and products than to talk about myself.

A few years ago, I hosted a multi-day event for women in Sonoma. One of the activities was an equine experience where we interacted with horses instead of riding them. Horses are one of the most intuitive creatures on earth and often show you what you are really communicating through your actions. Our group did a variety of exercises together and separately and the messages were powerful. We learned so much about ourselves by the way the horses interacted with us, or not.

In one significant activity, I found myself blocked off from the women as the horse was between me and them. The equine facilitator helped me interpret the experience, and in that moment, a light went off, my vulnerability was revealed, and I had a completely different outlook about myself, my work, and how I present myself to the world.

The bottom line was that I needed to get out from behind the horse. Throughout my life, I have been hiding, not so much from others, more from myself. I came from a large family, always feeling like I did not have my own voice and identity. I was hiding behind a 2,000-pound horse and I did not realize how much it affected me until that moment.

Those that know me well agree that I am a very private person, at times to a fault. It is something I have experienced as long as I can remember. It has not served me well, and in many ways has held me back from being my true self. What I found ironic in the equine experience is that through my vulnerability, I made a greater connection to the group as their leader. I was there *with* them, not talking *at* them. My vulnerability and realizations allowed for the group to also dig deep in their own profound way.

This experience, and many more moments like them in my life, are the stories I share in this book. It became my way of illuminating my truth and uncovering what matters most to me. Growing up it was "family first" and I felt I got lost in the shuffle. I kept my light dim and simply did what was right for the family. Yet, to fully embrace my place with them, and in the world, I needed to shine bright for myself.

INTRODUCTION

My grandparents and parents were the all-stars, my beacons of light, and they often imparted their wisdom to me through their storytelling. The best way I know to communicate what I learned from them is through re-telling their stories and sharing my experiences with them. I also tell my own stories and communicate my life lessons throughout the book.

This time of "great pause" allowed me to get out of my own way long enough to reflect on my memories and write them down. I felt like it was a perfect time to share my journey of finding myself and getting back to my roots.

Rooted in Family is ultimately my story, coming from two entrepreneurial families, working in the family business and finding my own way. I share the importance of honoring family roots and striving for family unity, especially in these modern and uncertain times. In a family, we need to nurture the off shoots to strengthen the roots, allowing the offshoots to grow and develop deeply on their own. This is the greatest gift I feel that I can give to my own children and the insight I can provide to others.

In order to remain rooted in my own family, I needed to find my own strength and my own identity. This brought a new sense of freedom to me as this was not a mindset I grew up with. Discovering my true self allowed me to find my passion and place in my family and the world, one of meaning and purpose.

I hope you enjoy reading my story as much as I enjoyed writing it.

Caroline.

ONE

Honoring the Past

"It was the best of times, it was the worst of times, it was the age of wisdom, it was the age of foolishness, it was the epoch of belief, it was the epoch of incredulity, it was the season of Light, it was the season of Darkness, it was the spring of hope, it was the winter of despair, we had everything before us, we had nothing before us, we were all going direct to Heaven, we were all going direct the other way—in short, the period was so far like the present period, that some of its noisiest authorities insisted on its being received, for good, or for evil, in the superlative degree of comparison only."

—Charles Dickens

This opening paragraph of Charles Dickens's book *A Tale of Two Cities* could very well describe the challenging year of 2020. Reflecting on all the world is going through in these unpredictable times, it seemed appropriate to get perspective from Dickens's dramatic historical fiction set in the time of the French Revolution.

We are in a transitional time, experiencing a global pandemic, and hopefully we will someday look back with reverence for all those who lost their lives or endured tremendous change. For better or for worse, there has been a shift in our culture and way of doing things that will likely result in a permanent change. We need to remember that our world has survived many challenging times, and we will rise again.

This transition has allowed me time to pause, reflect, discover, appreciate, and get back to what is important in life—the people, places and things worth valuing. I have appreciated the gift of getting back to basics and the simple pleasures of life.

Being sheltered in place at home has reinforced the importance of being "rooted in family." Without distractions of the complicated modern world, I have been able to reflect on my life, realizing hindsight truly is 2020. I have navigated my way through simple and complex times, low points and high points—ones that brought me great joy and ones that brought me "the other way." I have also learned that some things that seemed important were not, while others were simple and most memorable.

This has been a culminating year for me personally and professionally. I have contemplated the unpredictable paths I took, the extraordinary experiences I chose, and the critical decisions I made shaping the course of my life and making me the person I am today.

Since I have always been a private person, sharing my story does not come easily. However, given this time of pause and all that we are going through, I feel the topic of family is relevant today more than ever and is the best time to share my journey.

The importance of family goes back to the dawn of time when family life shaped societies around the globe in different cultures, languages, and circumstances. Families helped us endure epidemics, wars, revolutions, and natural disasters. The roots of family are challenged and tested over time. Having solid roots is paramount, especially today during these difficult and unsettling times. It is the strength of our roots that keeps us grounded, connected, and sustained for generations to come.

Remembering those who have passed helps me reflect and appreciate the present moment. Up until now my life has been filled with busyness. Sheltering in place, pausing, and slowing down in this new global reality has been a big leap for me. As I grew up, chaos became the norm—I was constantly on the go, filled with nervous energy, and often engaged in unnecessary activity. That pattern continued…until now.

Slowing down has provided the opportunity to be intentional in my actions, celebrating the "present" of the precious present. I have relished getting back to basics and enjoying simple pleasures like rocking in chairs with nowhere to be, watching the grass grow, listening to the wind in the trees while feeling the warmth of a bright sunny day.

Coming from a large family, it was always a pleasure to enjoy quality time alone with my Grandmother Aileen and Grandfather Julio at their home. I am forever grateful for my experiences there. I can remember following them around their garden, collecting eggs from the chicken coop, picking ripe beauties off fruit trees, plucking fresh discoveries from the veggie garden, and learning about every species of plants, trees and flowers.

My grandparents, Julio and Aileen, in their garden

A highlight I always enjoyed, and one that I recreate today, is embracing an active and exciting kitchen. I saved my hand-written notes and recipes and shared them with my children so they could also enjoy them and create new traditions. I was inspired by the sounds of chopping, talking, conversing, and plotting how to make a certain dish just right. I loved the smell of fresh herbs, fruits, and simmering delights. I enjoyed tasting, savoring, watching so intently, and making notes so as not to forget a tip not found in the recipe. I suppose that is why I have such an olfactory experience at the smell of fresh mint, basil, and other herbs, fresh flowers, plants, and trees. It takes me back to a childlike place, a sweet and tender time.

My grandparents helped me appreciate homegrown, homemade, generosity, compassion, and taking pleasure in the simple things of life. One of my most significant memories is of my Grandmother Aileen impressing on us the importance of family unity. She often shared a reminder of this at meals, after a prayer, or at family gatherings. It has come to a point where unity is not talked about in our family—we just live it. These two small words—*family unity*—have motivated me throughout my life, and unity is a legacy I am inspired to leave for my own family.

In a rare moment at the end of a family meeting, my Grandmother Aileen stood, pointed her fingers up, and said, "Good soil, good grapes, and family unity." Then she sat right down. She unknowingly played the role of the "Chief Emotional Officer," the glue holding us together as a family. She is an inspiration to me in many ways, which is why I am so passionate about family unity.

An iconic photo of my Grandmother Aileen at a family meeting

Because of her influence on me and my extended family around the importance of family unity, I wrote a poem for her the day she died, July 21, 1999. What I remember most vividly is how easily the words came to me. Within minutes of learning of her passing, the words flowed so naturally, it was as if she was right there with me in spirit helping me write it just so. I wrote it for myself and eventually shared it with my family, reading it at her funeral. Little did I know at the time how important her plea for family unity would be and how it would linger on in my family today.

Family Unity Forever

Family Unity is what you have always praised, with your pointed fingers of strength, we will always crave.

Your love and passion for life is as contagious as your smile, your poise and grace are something we will always admire.

You are a great example to us all, so giving of yourself, that others would have abundance, never thinking of yourself.

You always preached Grandpa's wish for good soil and good grapes, but your desire for Family Unity will live on in our hearts everyday.

Because of your good example and passion for this plea, Family Unity forever we will always be.

—Caroline Coleman Bailey, July 21, 1999

Honoring the past with respect and appreciation allows the opportunity to experience the future in a new and different way. It brings hope for simpler times and perspective for a better and brighter future, providing a lasting gift for generations to come.

TWO

A Tale of Two Families

Drawing further inspiration from Dickens's *A Tale of Two Cities* I had an opportunity to compare and contrast the two families into which I was born. While my story does not have the same dark drama as the Dickens's novel, I have come to realize families are families. They may have different roots, a different cast of characters, and different issues, yet they often prove to be more similar than different no matter where one goes in the world.

Two Entrepreneurial Families

I was born into two entrepreneurial families, both of whom came from very humble beginnings. Both histories have had great impact on me in different ways, and although one is now more visible than the other, there are commonalities. This is a story of growing up in two strong families and two strong businesses, and the challenges, rewards, and lessons I experienced along the way.

The entrepreneurial story on my mother's side started with two brothers, Ernest and Julio Gallo, born in 1909 and 1910, the sons of Italian immigrants who struggled to make a living farming grapes in California. With the advent of Prohibition in the 1920s, the market for selling grapes became difficult. Both brothers worked incessantly for their disciplinarian father, and through that experience they developed a bond and work ethic that would endure for their lifetimes.

In the early 1930s, two pivotal things happened. First, their parents passed away dramatically and left the two brothers a small vineyard in central California. Second, Prohibition was repealed in 1933. Despite not knowing anything about how to make wine, and not having any capital, they decided to start a winery, and the Ernest and Julio Gallo Winery was born. Ernest focused on sales and marketing while Julio concentrated on growing grapes and making wine. Their partnership was summed up by their commitment to each other—"I'll sell as much wine as you can make," and "I'll make as much wine as you can sell."

Today, the story of their beginnings may sound simple— two brothers with different areas of skill honoring each other's areas of expertise—although they were difficult and complex times. From the book *Ernest & Julio—Our Story*, published in 1994, Julio stated, "Going through the Depression tended to make a person cautious about money and land. From the beginning, Ernest and I were very conservative in business. That never changed through the years. I can tell you we've always made every dollar count."

When I think about it, I am amazed at how much the odds were stacked against them. It was a huge risk for two brothers with nothing more than a high school education, a vineyard, and very little cash to start a winery after the repeal of Prohibition. And that was not all—they knew nothing about making wine. There was no way to Google the information they needed. So where did they go? The public library.

According to *Our Story*, Ernest shared

> I went to the Modesto library to look for a book on winemaking. I told the librarian what I had in mind, but she found nothing on the shelves. After all, we were just ending more than a decade of national Prohibition, during which there had been no call for winemaking literature. As I turned to leave, she remembered some old pamphlets in the basement. I went downstairs and found a stack of magazines and pamphlets. I went through it and found a pamphlet on fermentation and one on the care of the wine by Professor Frederic T. Bioletti of the Department of Viticulture and Enology at the University of California at Davis, published prior to Prohibition. This was the beginning of our knowledge about making commercial wine, such as how to have a sound, clean fermentation, and how to clarify the wine. These old pamphlets probably saved us from going out of business our very first year.

In spite of finding this valuable information, had we taken a personal inventory at that time, our prospects would have looked very dismal:

Experience in producing commercial wine: none.
Experience in marketing wine: none.
Available cash: $900.23.
Borrowed funds: $5,000.

But I would have added this important intangible:

Confidence: Unbounded!

Why was I so confident? Because at the time, all of twenty-four years of age, I honestly felt that I could do anything anyone else could do—not because I was brilliant or well-educated, but because I was willing to devote as much time and effort as was necessary, regardless of the sacrifice. And I knew that my brother Julio, equally dedicated to doing a good job, would make a dependable, hardworking partner. Though others underestimated our capacities, Julio and I did not.

In *Our Story*, Julio shared

Ernest sold all our wine that first year. There was no letup at all from our busy fall and winter. No vacation or days off for either of us—just work and more work, seven days a week. And they were long days.

Sometimes, after working eighteen hours, we would be called out in the middle of the night and go down to the winery because of some problem. We were going to make damn sure that we didn't fail.

Our wives recognized the pressure we were under. They put up with our long hours and supported us in every way possible. While Amelia helped out at the winery, Aileen ran the household, cooking and cleaning. They both worked very hard, and never complained.

Come fall, Ernest and I decided to expand the winery. We had survived the first round, which I credit to the toughness of youth and our willingness to work hard. To expand for that second season we needed more grapes, more equipment and tanks, more of everything.

A major concern was acquiring additional cooperage, which was expensive and in demand, owing to all the new wineries starting up. When we asked Pacific Redwood Company of San Francisco for more cooperage on credit terms, the owner of the company, an old German named Schmidt, came to Modesto to check us out. I took Schmidt through the winery—our rented warehouse was getting crowded—and pointed out where we would install the new cooperage.

Schmidt took it all in, then asked me where I lived.

"We live on a ranch out on Maze Road," I said.

"Can we go out and take a look?"

"Sure."

We drove out Maze Road and I gave him a tour of the vineyards. The 160 acres across the street that Ernest and I worked and planted four years earlier had come into full production the previous year.

We pulled into the yard behind the house, and went in the back door. Aileen was in the kitchen trying to make lunch, and our baby, Bob, just a month old, was in his crib crying. There she was with her hands full, and there I am arriving with an unexpected guest for lunch.

Without hesitation, Schmidt reached into the crib and picked up our baby, explaining, "Oh, I know about babies." He began pacing back and forth, patting Bob gently on the back. Soon, little Bob was quiet. When Schmidt bent over and placed him back in his crib, our son was sound asleep.

"We raised four kids," he said. "They grow up so fast."

Through lunch, Schmidt didn't talk business at all. Instead, he chatted mostly about kids, family life with my wife. He was obviously a good-hearted, down-to-earth guy, which I appreciated, but while he was talking to Aileen, all I could think about was am I going to get the tanks?

After lunch we drove back to town. On the ride, I started to bring up the subject of more cooperage.

Schmidt stopped me short. "I have a cooper putting in tanks at another winery. When he's finished, I'll have him come over to your place. Don't worry, you'll have your tanks. You pay me when you can."

That was that. Schmidt had found a hardworking family man, and he could see that Ernest and I were determined to succeed. He decided that E. & J. Gallo Winery was worth taking a chance on.

It was the way business was done back then. Get to know a man and trust what you see. Gain each other's confidence, and seal the deal on your word and a handshake.

I miss those days.

As early as 1934, my Grandfather Julio was traveling to Sonoma and Napa developing relationships with vintners and growers. He often said, "Quality fruit produces quality wines." I believe his secret was the strong business and personal relationships he made and closing a deal with a handshake. This "heart of the deal" proved to be his hallmark, connecting and building rapport within the industry. No matter who you were, he treated you with respect and fairness. This proved successful in setting up long-term contracts, which were unheard of at the time. This guaranteed pricing to growers in such a volatile business. Many of his practices are continued today and were built from curiosity and solid "common-sense farming." Over the years, several of our vineyard and winery properties have been acquired through these practices and through families doing business with other families.

Both Ernest and Julio refused mediocrity and always strived for perfection, with the goal of providing the consumer with top-quality wine at affordable prices. Anything is possible, especially when the odds are against you, and for Ernest and Julio they were. With determination, hard work, and steadfast commitment to quality and excellence, the business became successful and steadily grew as did their families, requiring us to change and adapt. In their lifetimes, Ernest and Julio saw their business transition from an entrepreneurial early-stage business led by two brothers to a professionally run business which transitioned to the second generation. With the third generation now at the helm, the business is going through another transition of keeping up with the needs and demands of the modern-day consumer. On the family side, it continues to grow, and there are also needs for a growing family, like good governance, particularly when not everyone works in the business.

The other entrepreneurial story is from my father's side, and it is also from humble beginnings. My dad is one of three boys born in Corvallis, Oregon, where his parents— my grandparents—were entrepreneurs who started A. E. Coleman Jewelers back in 1927. This was not a typical mom-and-pop business. Their story, particularly given the current global pandemic, is fascinating and gives more perspective of their time.

My grandfather, Alfred Coleman, contracted polio five years before the United States had its first major outbreak in 1916 and fifty years before the first safe anti-polio vaccine was made available in 1961.

In his book *Sticks*, published posthumously by my father and his brothers in his honor in 2004, Alfred shared,

> At the age of nine, I was playing hide-and-go-seek one summer evening, a very popular children's game that involves a lot of running about. It wasn't long until the calves of my legs began to hurt. I was sent to bed, and

the next day when I awoke, the doctor and my mother were standing over me.

"I'm sorry, but there is nothing I can do for him," the doctor said.

Little did I know that polio was my illness or how it would affect my future.

It was then that I first had the feeling of being helpless. Like most children, I had taken arms, legs, and hands for granted, and I thought them just something to kick and scratch with. For a few days, I couldn't move either of my hands, legs, or my head off the pillow. I don't recall how long it was before I began to improve, but as I look back now, each day seemed a year.

As I began to improve, I had to learn to crawl and walk all over again. I couldn't seem to keep from falling down, and my knees always seemed to give way and let me go down in a heap.

The book goes on to explain:

Alfred he was lucky. Because his case was early for his region—it was believed to be the first reported in his county—there was no panic or stigma attached to the disease. Unlike in New York City, where the 1916 epidemic struck 27,000 people and killed

6,000, people in Myrtle Creek, Oregon, weren't being quarantined and criminally prosecuted if they violated public-health rules. Nobody put a sign on the Coleman family home saying, "Infantile Paralysis—Beware." Indeed, if neighbors looked upon Alfred with anything but sympathy, he never spoke of it.

Alfred Coleman was also fortunate to be living in a sparsely populated farming region of western Oregon, far from the hospital wards where many city kids with polio were sent to live. The polio wards were sad places. They were crowded and noisy, not with the din of children's voices, but with the constant whooshing of the iron lungs. Nurses were few, partly to limit spread of the disease. Individual attention was rare and often more dutiful than caring. Visitors told of seeing huge rooms full of lonely children with tears in their eyes. Alfred's experience was nothing like this. His mother, Emma, was always close at hand to comfort his suffering, of which there was plenty.

Imagine running around as a child one day and then the next day waking up with polio and being unable to walk for the rest of your life. While a story like this could send many people into a downward spiral, especially with the stigma associated with polio in the early 1900s, my grandfather never let this set him back. He called his crutches "sticks." He did not want sympathy from others. In fact, when he traveled in airports, he never requested a wheelchair to get him to the airline gate—he preferred to use his "sticks."

My Grandfather Alfred was the very picture of triumph over disability. Despite contracting polio at the age of nine, he went on to become a true renaissance man. He accomplished many things—he was a champion archer, expert musician, guitar maker, woodcarver, singer, bird caller and whistler, poet, skilled watchmaker, and owner of a successful jewelry business. He was highly creative and was dedicated to his business, his family, and his passions.

He even wrote the book *Sticks*, a book about his accomplishments while overcoming the debilitating effects of polio. The book was accepted by most VA hospital libraries in the United States.

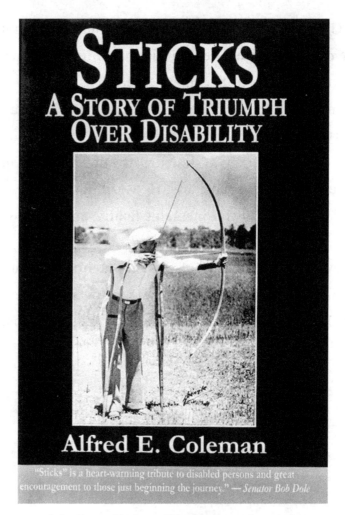

*My Grandfather Alfred's tripod stance
on the cover of his book Sticks*

He and my Grandmother Vera encouraged me to visit their home in Oregon, and as a young girl I observed this remarkable couple in their jewelry store, getting a glimpse of their working life. She was a very modern woman in her day as she managed their family jewelry store while raising three boys. She was an early model of a working mom, and she opened my eyes to this possibility.

My Grandparents Alfred and Vera

One of the poems I found in his things after his passing epitomizes my Grandfather Alfred. It emphasizes the importance of the person staring back from the "glass." Although it was originally written from the masculine point of view, it can have the same meaning for women.

The Man in the Glass

When you get what you want in your struggle for self
And the world makes you king for the day
Just go to the mirror and look at yourself
And see what the man has to say.

For it isn't your father, or mother, or wife
Whose judgement upon you must pass
The fellow whose verdict counts most in your life
Is the one staring back from the glass.
He's the fellow to please-never mind all the rest
For he's with you, clear to the end
And you've passed your most difficult, dangerous test
If the man in the glass is your friend.
You may fool the whole world down the pathway of years
And get pats on the back as you pass
But your final reward will be heartache and tears
If you've cheated the man in the glass.

—Peter Dale Wimrow Sr., 1934

My Grandfather Alfred was someone I really looked up to. Being less mobile because of his "sticks" allowed him to take things more slowly. I found comfort in his presence, his patience, and his natural ability to spend quality time whenever we were together. As a little girl, I remember he always had time for me, whether it was unraveling my delicate knotted-up necklace in no time, to happily brushing my hair when no-one else was available. One of my favorite memories was listening to him sing and play his favorite tunes on his guitar, including Roger Miller's "Little Green Apples" and "King of the Road." I can still hear those songs ringing in my head from time to time as I think of him strumming and singing with his guitar on his lap.

His life was cut short, just as my Grandfather Julio's was. Both died unexpectedly. I was seven years old when my Grandfather Alfred passed. Those seven precious years I did have with him were the most impressionable and magical.

Both sets of grandparents had profound impact on my life. Although their stories of humble beginnings are different, they influenced me in similar ways. What I gained from their stories and presence was an innate sense of wisdom, appreciation for life, value of hard work, ability to overcome adversity, and the power of family.

A rare photo of my two grandfathers together, Alfred and Julio

A rare photo of my two grandmothers together, Vera and Aileen

Both my parents are accomplished and entrepreneurial as well. They encouraged my entrepreneurial spirit and instilled in me everything it took to succeed in my own endeavors. They were college sweethearts who have been married sixty-three years, raised eight children, and are proud grandparents of twenty-eight grandchildren and eighteen great-grandchildren (with more on the way). While raising a family this size is an accomplishment in itself, my parents also pursued their own interests with immense success, strongly devoted to their faith and always giving back to the community.

My parents, Jim and Sue in Burgundy, France

My dad, James Coleman, said his parents, Alfred and Vera, taught him and his two brothers how to persevere—even in the face of devastating odds. During their many years of working in their jewelry store while growing up, they were taught what it takes to build a successful family business, to be an achiever, to always be honest, and to get along with people. My dad applied these traits through his many years of progressing to become a co-president of E. & J. Gallo Winery. He learned how to produce high-quality wine, make good decisions, and strive for continuous improvement every step of the way. He upheld the vision of Ernest and Julio and showed all of us in our family that drive, passion, and deeply rooted values lead to success.

In addition to his leadership in the family business, my dad is also a prominent cattle rancher, starting Vintage Angus in 1976 breeding generations of high-end black angus cattle. His interest in cattle was sparked during his many visits as a boy to his uncle Herb Coleman's Jersey dairy. Herb Coleman was a leading dairyman in Oregon and was president of the Oregon Jersey Association. There was something noble and special about Herb's work, instilling values that drove my dad to rediscover that farming was in his blood.

Two of my four brothers worked one summer on a commercial Angus ranch. They came home to return to high school and said to my dad, "We should have some Angus cattle around our home ranch."

Dad replied, "If you build the fence, I will buy the Angus cows."

The boys persuaded him to go to Ankony Angus in Loyalton, California, to buy some cows. This led to the first purchase of four females and the beginning of Vintage Angus. His vision of "producing the ultimate Angus genetics" generated enormous advances in the industry. Vintage Angus benefitted greatly from teaming up the best minds in the Angus world with my dad's business mind to make an unbeatable combination. The results speak for themselves.

My dad is not only a force in business, he is a force in our family and an influence in my own success. He encouraged me to listen, participate in business discussions, and bring my own ideas to the table. His encouragement drove me to work hard in the family business and continuously strive to be the best version of myself.

Like my grandmother, my mother—Susann Gallo Coleman—was the glue that held our family together. She raised eight children—a business in itself—and sparked her own entrepreneurial spirit in antiques that outgrew our home. She had a passion for collecting them for as long as I can remember. When there were too many to display in our home, she started an antique shop locally in Modesto and eventually opened Garden Court Antiques in the San Francisco Design Center. She has been an avid collector of fine European antiques for more than fifty years. She focused on early English furniture and expanded to late seventeenth-eighteenth-and nineteenth-century European furniture and decorative arts. In her years of travel throughout Europe, she began to see that quality had less to do with a specific country or period and more to do with the individual piece. Her passion for extraordinary pieces, combined with her exceptional taste, brought warmth and elegance to her business and our home.

The quality of the patina, the shape, the color, the texture and most importantly the soul of the objects themselves captivated her attention. She finds the story behind the pieces she collects, and takes great pride in sharing them with family, customers, and admirers, bringing life to the pieces each time she shares their story. She is gifted with an eye for detail and ability to discover the "find." When asked what she looks for when shopping around the globe, her response is, "I look for pieces that have soul. I can't really describe what that means exactly, but I know it when I see it!" Her sense of style, eye for detail, appreciation of quality, and love of travel are all gifts I received from my mom.

My family celebrating my mom's birthday

The entrepreneurial spirit of my parents rubbed off on me and my siblings, so much so that seven of the eight have their own businesses today. In my own firm, Premier Growth, The Business of Family® is a concept rooted in the large family into which I was born. As long as I can remember, there was constant activity around. The need for order, structure, discipline, and routine was a necessary part of managing the "organized chaos." Running a large family is like running a small business—at least it was in my family's household while I was growing up. Watching and learning as my parents managed eight children, instilling the importance of planning and organization, was my introduction to professionalizing the family.

My Grandfather Julio, teaching me and
my siblings a lesson in discipline

My legacy is found with all my family, past and present. I am blessed to be surrounded by entrepreneurs who have generously given of their time, talent, and treasure while playing many different roles in my life. These special people have guided and shaped me into the person I am today.

THREE

The Shade of the Family Tree

"For all the people of the earth, the Creator has planted a Sacred Tree under which they may gather, and there find healing, power, wisdom and security. The roots of this tree spread deep into the body of Mother Earth. Its branches reach upward like hands praying to Father Sky. The fruits of this tree are the good things the Creator has given to the people: teachings that show the path to love, compassion, generosity, patience, wisdom, justice, courage, respect, humility, and many other wonderful gifts."

—Four Worlds International Institute

In many cultures around the world, trees are very symbolic. The tree is a place of gathering, especially for communities, providing a central place for communing together and casting much-needed shade of comfort, especially in hot temperatures.

What, then, is "The Shade of the Family Tree?" Just as a tree grows and expands, a family grows and expands from its seedling (first-generation family) to its vast branches (succeeding generations). The life of the tree shows in its leaves and changes throughout the seasons. With the right nutrients—soil, sunlight, air, and water—its roots solidly expand into the earth, and branches grow out and up to the sky while the tree gets taller and wider over the years until shade cascades from the tree. For a family, the tree creating shade becomes "home," a safe place to meet, relax, enjoy, learn, and grow together as a family.

Trees hold a lot of meaning for me, especially since I came from an agricultural family, where trees were all around— ranches, vineyard properties and homes. Trees are in my DNA. With trees, there was purpose, security, and beauty. Trees even provided pleasure as we enjoyed climbing, swinging on, sitting under, watching the glistening leaves, and listening to the delightful sounds.

As I grew up under the shade of the family tree and branched out, little did I know then how two key decisions would change the course of my life.

Growing Up

My secret hope and desire was to be an only child so I could have the full attention of my parents and be surrounded by peace and quiet. Instead, I was born into a large family. I am one of eight children in my family, with four boys and four girls. I am child number five, the youngest of the "first family" and the oldest of the "second family." What that means is that the first five were born very close together, followed by a five-year break after me and the next three siblings.

We did not have a lot of forms of entertainment that we have today. We relied on being out in nature. We rarely watched television, and when we did, it was a special occasion mostly focused on family shows we watched together on a Friday, Saturday, or Sunday night. We also played a lot of family games together both indoors and outdoors, from cards and board games to swimming, tennis, and football.

My Family—Mom, Dad, Chris, Greg, Brad, Joan,
Caroline, Ted, Tim, Anne
1976

When I look back on my early childhood—spending considerable time outside on the ranch doing chores, with no screen time—I do not recall any time that I was bored. In fact, the opposite was true. It was my nature to find fun in most things, even in menial tasks. I remember pulling pranks on my older sister Joan—it was the jokester in me. After having another sisterly squabble, Mom assigned us our usual penance of pulling weeds. She took us outside and stated, "Joan, you start here and go to that rock— Caroline, you follow behind her from that rock to this stick. Now have at it and don't come in until it's done." While pulling weeds deep in thought, curious how to make it fun, I found worms and flicked them with a stick in my sister's direction. She was unaware where they were coming from until she realized it was me, and of course the sisterly battles began—again.

I also found myself getting creative and making use of the things around me, many of them in arts and craft projects. I loved arts and crafts and spent much time collecting and gathering things of insignificance that I would formulate into something special, sometimes not knowing ahead of time what that would be. I remember once finding a wire hanger and telling my mom, "Hold on to this—I want to make something out of it when I get home from school." Mom had a confused look on her face, having no idea what would become of this wire hanger that I pleaded with her to hold on to until I returned. Sure enough, when I got home, I found some fabric and glue and made a hat out of the hanger to her surprise and delight. She became used to my simple requests, and the creative things I made from ordinary things around the house. This became my way of life, with no questions asked. Visioning, transforming, and thinking outside the box came naturally to me.

Off to preschool

When it came time for my science project in high school, I knew exactly what I wanted to do. I declared I wanted to make wine, and no one seemed surprised. It felt like a logical choice for me and reflected my early interest in the family business. I recall many times when my sisters and mother cleared the table after dinner and went to the kitchen to clean up while I stayed at the family dinner table with my dad, Grandfather Julio, my brothers, and often visiting business executives. Being truly interested in their conversation, I got lost in it while my sisters thought I was simply unwilling to clean up. For me, this was not the case at all. I was learning from the stories they were sharing. This knowledge and information became ingrained in me through osmosis. It was more than just being a fly on the wall—it was learning from their stories and treasuring every moment.

Dad, who was well-aware of my interest, became my biggest advocate in making wine for my project. I was not aware of any rules at the time about the legal drinking age—it was just part of our family and business. As I pondered what part of the wine process I would center my project around, Dad and I came up with the idea of fermenting white wine at two different temperatures—one warm and one cool—and determining which method made a better wine. There were four tasters as judges—two professional tasters (my father and Grandfather Julio) and two "experienced" tasters (my mother and Grandmother Aileen).

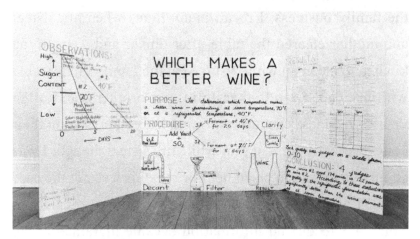

My high school science project

This science project solidified my interest in science, balancing my artistic and creative side. It was at this time that our family business piqued my interest.

The second time I made wine was during a summer high-school internship at the winery. My Grandfather Julio told me, "If you want to learn about wine, you need to make it." I took his advice to heart, and I went through the entire process of making wine that summer of 1981. I hand-picked the grapes with help from my cousin Tom. The only grape variety ready for harvest before I had to go back to school was Sauvignon Blanc. We picked the grapes in Livingston, just south of Modesto, and I brought them back to our mini-winery, the "Pilot Plant," where I crushed them, went through each step in making wine, bottled the wine, and hand-corked the bottles. I even designed a label, since I also worked in the Creative Services Department that summer, and I gave a bottle to both Ernest and my Grandfather Julio for Christmas.

The Sauvignon Blanc wine I made
during the summer of 1981

Making my wine from grape to glass was a memorable and educational experience that confirmed my passion for science and art. I will never forget my grandfather's reaction—he said it was one of the best Sauvignon Blanc wines he had tasted. (I knew he was being a very generous and gracious grandfather.) Going through the process was a real learning experience for me, and I am forever grateful.

It also verified my decision that I did not want to become a winemaker like he wanted me to, and it was difficult to tell him that. I felt strongly there was something else out there for me, though I was just not sure what it was.

Branching Out

I knew I would be going off to school soon and would need to make a choice as to which area of study to select. I remember being completely undecided, although I knew exactly which university I wanted to attend. I had visited the University of Southern California with a family friend and stayed with her on campus, and I immediately knew I had made my choice. Now to convince the university and my family.

I was quite active in high school in sports and many extracurricular activities, and I had good grades. My parents encouraged me to apply to more than one university in case I did not get accepted, even though I had decided on one school. It did not occur to me that I might not be accepted, as I was so driven and knew where I wanted to attend. Deep down I knew I had the grades, scores, and activities needed. Would that be enough? In the spring, when acceptance letters were sent out from universities, I went to the mailbox every day, waiting for my acceptance letters. I'll never forget finally seeing a letter with the return address *University of Southern California*. I paused slightly, closed my eyes, opened the letter slowly, and read that I had been accepted. I jumped in the air, smiling from ear to ear, so happy. I did it!

This was one of the first major decisions I made on my own, venturing outside the shade of the family tree. The decision to go to Los Angeles did not go over well at first with my family—my older siblings all went to universities close to home. To my family, it must have felt like I was going to South America. All they knew is it seemed far away, and from what they heard, it was dangerous. It was a bold step for me and one that paved the way for other family members to attend the same school, so perhaps my choice was fortuitous. Looking back now, it had a tremendous effect on me.

That fall I packed and loaded my car—had it not been for my high school fundraiser where my parents purchased a car the year before, I would not have had one. Purchases in our family had purpose. My parents and grandparents on both sides taught us the value of money and hard work, and that is one of the greatest gifts I received from their humble beginnings. This value is difficult to teach in this day and age with everything a click away.

Grandmother Aileen seeing me off

I drove on my own to the heart of downtown Los Angeles, I had no GPS, no Google maps, no apps, no cell phone and was totally oblivious to any safety issues I would face along the way. Though I did get lost as I got nearer to campus, the excitement drove me to my new school, and I moved into my new home away from home—the dorm. Looking back, it never occurred to me why my parents were not helping me move to university. I did not expect them to take me. I grew up in a large family where seniority ruled. I was child number five, and that was the filter I lived by. Independence and taking initiative started early, so I was accustomed to doing things on my own. This was not a time of helicopter parenting—in fact, it was the opposite.

Arriving at USC with an undeclared major, I immediately immersed myself in leadership activities and realized I liked communicating and interacting with people. After taking courses in a variety of areas, I decided to major in communications. I knew this would not go over well with my Grandfather Julio, as he was quite eager for me to become a winemaker. I stood firm in my decision and remember sharing it with him on one of his trips to Los Angeles to visit me and my older sister Joan who transferred to USC. I could only imagine pursuing a career I enjoyed and found meaningful.

Working in the Family Business

After graduating with a communications degree from USC, I did not go into the family business right away, much to my family's surprise. In fact, before I graduated, I had applied for a long-shot job and was excited to be one of eight chosen to represent my sorority, Kappa Alpha Theta, on a national level as a Chapter Consultant. It was my first job and involved a one-year commitment, living out of a suitcase and visiting universities across the country. We were each assigned a territory of universities—mine was the Midwest and the Northeast.

I loved all aspects of this role—it represented freedom for me to travel, see the country, and work with people. It felt like an extra year of university and offered a new reason to be back on campus. I met with chapter leadership and heads of universities, and reported to our national headquarters in Indianapolis, Indiana. The job involved long hours and grueling travel, and I loved every moment. The year passed quickly, and I was sad it was only a one-year commitment. This was the beginning of my consulting days—it has resonated with me ever since. As my year was coming to a close, I started to contemplate my next opportunity.

I remember early on receiving some unsolicited advice: Find something you love to do, and figure out a way to make a living out of it, and you will never work a day in your life. I really liked to travel, I loved working with people, and I still had a deep interest in working in the family business. I was just not sure how I would leverage my degree in communications.

I moved back to my hometown of Modesto and applied to work in our family business, and I was offered a position in the Public Relations Department. It seemed like a good fit and logical step given my interest and education. My role was entry level, mostly desk work and phone calls. It soon evolved into an opportunity to work closely with Ernest for the first time. This new project provided visibility for our fine wines to high-end consumers at special events in two key markets—San Francisco and Los Angeles. I remember Ernest was directly involved in setting standards for visibility of our wines at these events, and my job was to enact the strict guidelines.

In my annual review, my supervisor recommended the best way to learn and grow my career in the business was to work in sales with my own territory. So after a year in the Public Relations Department, I accepted a position to work in the hotel and restaurant division for our San Francisco Bay Area distributor at the time, Gallo Sales Company. My territory was downtown San Francisco, one of the most difficult markets since we had limited premium wines available. One of the wines we reintroduced was our 1978 Cabernet Sauvignon as an upscale option for hotels and restaurant wine lists. We had a limited quantity of the wine, which was unusual for our wines at that time, and required a sit-down educational tasting, in which we often beat better-known fine wines in blind tastings. Discerning sommeliers discovered this to be a true collectors' wine.

After working for a year in the challenging downtown San Francisco territory while increasing sales and calling on key accounts, our vice president of international sales asked to meet with me in San Francisco. He told me the company was expanding our wine sales to Canada and asked if I would be interested in a position there. I was quite pleased and delighted for the opportunity, although it was not something I had discussed with my family— especially my parents. I wondered how they would react to the idea of their daughter moving to Canada. I remember enthusiastically agreeing to next steps that included several interviews, including one with the lead manager of Canada. They were looking for someone who could train a new team of sales representatives for our wines and also call on national hotel and restaurant accounts. I was up for the challenge and felt confident I could do the job, especially given my experience in the San Francisco market. The bigger obstacle was how to tell my family. The assignment was one I was excited about, and I let this excitement be my motivation.

After receiving the job offer, I went home and told my parents that I had accepted a job in Canada. It was a surprise to them, and they were not pleased at first. For them, I might as well have been moving to the North Pole. I recall my parents speculating I would marry a Canadian and they would never see me again. I suppose I subliminally took that in and soon discovered their speculation would become somewhat true.

We are a close-knit family. Growing up with family all around becomes the norm, comfortable and secure. That is the feeling of comfort and warmth under the shade of the family tree. When family is not there, wonder sets in and can easily become fear, wanting to make sure everyone is safe and healthy. This is especially true for the older generations, including my parents. Now as a mother, I understand about the care and concern of family, especially my own. I always want to know that everyone is safe and healthy, although sometimes my children may think otherwise.

Uncharted Territory

From as early as I can remember, I studied maps as a child, and I was fascinated by the bright colors, shapes, names, and vastness of the global world. This piqued my interest in international endeavors, and Canada was my first step. The adventurer in me was sparked. At that point, I had no idea how it would change the course of my life. This second big decision, after going to university in Los Angeles, was where I grew my wings.

So, in 1989, I made the move to Canada to build the market there, training local sales representatives and calling on hotel and restaurant national accounts. Later, I also worked on marketing and public relation endeavors in Canada as well as traveling to meet with press and media in other countries around the world.

When I arrived in Toronto, I did not know a soul. I landed with suitcase in hand and was put in touch with a real estate agent to assist me in finding an apartment. I enjoyed working for the family business, especially internationally, as it was a time of growing and expanding into new territory, which fed my entrepreneurial spirit.

My work in Canada spanned the country, and I think I saw more of Canada than most Canadians. It was satisfying to have our wines received so well. My focus was selling our wines to hotels and restaurants as the import option. I remember calling on a national hotel chain that was placing a large order and hearing them say, "We haven't heard of your wines. Do you think you can supply us with the quantities we need?"

Maintaining my composure, I enthusiastically replied "Yes, we can definitely supply you with the quantities you need!"

I also recall being on a ride with a sales representative I was training, and the conversation veered to him asking me if I knew who Wayne Gretsky was. When I asked, "Who is that?" he abruptly yet safely pulled off the side of the road to a dead stop, and in a shocked and surprised tone said, "You don't know who Wayne Gretsky is?" It was as if I had done something sacrilegious by not knowing this holy grail of hockey. I soon became familiar with the many talented Canadians in sports, music, entertainment, and beyond, including local lingo, culture, currency, and a country so different from my own.

I fell in love with Canada—the land, the people, and the Indigenous culture. I was living life physically, emotionally, and mentally on the outside looking in at the United States and viewing it in a whole new perspective. It was eye-opening experience. For example, learning how people made their wine decisions was revealing. Advertising alcohol was not allowed in Canada then, so wine consumers had to read about wines from the recommendations of wine writers and reviewers or through tastings at wine festivals and events. For me, it was a real culture shift.

I did meet and marry "my Canadian," thanks to my real estate agent-turned-friend who introduced us, and I am forever grateful to her. In 1991, we were married and soon started a family, with our first child born in Toronto in 1993. Canada quickly became home. A Canadian cultural legacy was born, and I found a new way of life as I discovered and enjoyed my family there.

I decided to take the working mother path, following my Grandmother Vera's example. We were determined that the birth of our first child was not going to change our lives. I remember a lengthy cross-country trip—or, as it was known, a "road show" called The Grape Outdoors—during which I promoted our wines in numerous cities across Canada. I knew I could not be away from my daughter that long, and I needed support while I was working. When I spoke to my mom about this trip she volunteered to come along to help with my daughter, and my Grandmother Aileen enthusiastically agreed to come too. It sounded great in the moment, although after further thought I could hear myself saying, "What was I thinking?"

Four generations of women as my entourage—my daughter, my mom, my grandmother, and me, all of us together— what would that look like? It was an experience, and of course it created all sorts of "fun." As just one example, trying to do a simple task like bathing my daughter elicited a lot of opinions—use the tub. No, the tub is too large. Use the sink. Be sure to hold her head. Wait, you need a towel. Wait, where is the soap? It is too slippery. Hold on to her—not like that, like this. It was quite hysterical. I am quite sure my daughter slept like a baby that night. The rest of us? Not so sure.

My colleague and mentor who traveled end-to-end with us and has traveled with me on many trips around the world, commented that this one was the most memorable. He even captured a rare photo of us together.

Four generations in Vancouver, British Columbia, at the beginning of our trip across Canada

This was a rewarding trip for me on many levels, as I got to enjoy my daughter while bringing meaning and purpose to my mom and grandmother, especially after the loss of Julio earlier that year in 1993.

In 1994, just as I was settling into my family roots in Canada, my husband was offered a job in San Francisco.

We made the decision to move back to the United States after working in Canada for five years.

I have fond memories of my Canadian family. They hold a special place in my heart.

My in-laws lived in Northern Ontario, so it was a commitment to travel there—and was an even bigger commitment when we moved to California. It was a welcome journey each summer to spend quality time with them, providing an opportunity for our children to create traditions with their grandparents, cousins, aunts, and uncles to treasure.

*My four children at their grandparent's cottage
in Northern Ontario, Canada*

In honor of their family roots, we experienced a new and different culture that had great influence on me and our children. My in-laws were special people, and even though they have passed, my appreciation and connection to them and their family endures.

Upon my return to the San Francisco Bay Area, I was anxious to get back to work and contemplated which area of the business would be best. There was a need to meet the growing demands of visitors at our "not open to the public" facilities. Given my background in sales, marketing, and public relations in Canada and other countries, it was a natural fit for me to work in Sonoma County at our winery in Healdsburg, California. Since we were breaking new ground there, it provided opportunity to contribute in a variety of areas, including marketing communications, hospitality, and public relations. It also provided the opportunity to work closely with Ernest on our Gallo of Sonoma brand and Estate Fine Wines.

I was responsible for many other behind-the-scenes initiatives with Ernest, such as the development of the Frei Ranch House, a meeting spot for trade hospitality, and other projects in developing areas he wanted to explore. This was the most fascinating time for me to work directly with Ernest on such interesting and meaningful projects, especially ones he was passionate about. I treasured this time with him, much like I had when as a little girl I sat at the family dinner table with my dad and Grandfather Julio, listening to their business discussions. I continued to learn in this same way from Ernest through projects as well as his interactions and experiences with fellow industry icons. I still hold those times close to my heart and am forever changed by them.

I remember presenting ideas, potential programs, and projects to Ernest, who always found the smallest weakness. Together, we sought solutions to make them even stronger. He was a master at this. It trained me to focus on the details—every detail. I remember his attention to detail in everything we did, whether it was on a photo shoot with him behind the camera or determining the best couch comfort and height for our visitors at our Frei Ranch House, the hub for trade guests at the time. As he told me, "If the couches are too comfortable, our guests will not want to leave, and if they are too stiff, they will not want to stay." I learned to seek perfection in my projects with Ernest, knowing it did not exist. He challenged me in ways I never imagined, asked a lot of questions, and took my learning to new heights through his cleverness and insightful genius. He was a true entrepreneur.

At the time we were not open to the public and did not have all the vineyard and winery properties we have today. It was a pivotal time and represented a huge shift for our company, growing our fine wine business, especially our Gallo of Sonoma wines. To introduce wines at significantly higher price points and in limited quantities required validation, especially to wine collectors, trade, press, and media.

The introduction of our fine wines required substantial education and required upgrades—both underground and above—to our Sonoma winery. The ability to produce fine wine in small-barrel batches and scale up was an impressive feat. I called it the "largest small winery in the world," meaning we had small-scale capability to large-scale capacity with state-of-the-art technology and skill, no matter what level wine was being made. I worked closely with my cousins—Gina as winemaker, now Vice President of Estate Winemaking, and Matt as vineyard and winery manager, now Vice President of Coastal Operations—as we initiated awareness of our fine wines that had started long ago when my Grandfather Julio first purchased grapes from the north coast in 1934.

Building personal and lasting relationships is something I learned from both Ernest and Julio. One of the highlights of my role in Sonoma was developing my relationship with "The Captain," as Bill Bowers was referred to, proprietor of Captain's Tavern Restaurant in Miami. I met him while visiting with wine writers in his restaurant. He shared his love for California wines and his desire to visit our vineyards and meet our winemakers someday. In return he promised to provide lunch—fresh stone crabs. After leaving his restaurant I did not think further of his offer as it did not seem realistic to carry fresh stone crabs on an airplane.

When I received word that The Captain was coming to California during harvest and requested to meet the winemakers, I was excited and nervous at the same time. It was rare for a customer to bring lunch—usually it was the other way around. Harvest is always busy with little time to spare. I was concerned I would need to scramble to get people to show up. I made the appeal to my cousins Matt and Gina along with the winemaking team to join us for a picnic lunch at Julio's tree. This was a special spot in the live oak tree grove on the Frei Ranch vineyard with plenty of shade for picnics and a beautiful view overlooking Dry Creek Valley. I knew they needed to eat, and I pleaded with them to join me and The Captain, who would be providing fresh stone crabs from Miami with hammer in hand. Thankfully, I was successful getting a handful of takers.

We had a delightful time under Julio's tree that first year. It left such a lasting impression for those attending that we made it an annual tradition during harvest each year.

He continued to make the trek with his fresh stone crabs, and the event has evolved, extending beyond our family business to a well-attended local industry event. The Captain recently passed, and his memory lives on in the heart of many who were blessed by his presence.

Memorable moments like this are plentiful—not only with trade customers, also with our partners, distributors, and employees, who have become like family. Their hard work and dedication over the years have made them lifelong advocates for our business and our products and a true testament to our family and leadership.

My time with Ernest and Julio was like receiving a graduate degree in business, with first-hand experiential learning proving to be most valuable in my work today. I kept reminding myself that these were two men with limited educations—high-school graduates from humble beginnings with wise philosophies—who become such extraordinary men accomplishing great things and building a household name for wine in the United States and around the world.

Ernest and my Grandfather Julio shared an entrepreneurial spirit. They were hard workers, used their common sense, paid close attention to detail, and were never satisfied. They had unwavering dedication to quality, always striving for perfection while remaining humble in the process. Their differences made them a great team—and the rest is history.

My Grandfather Julio lived to see his dream come true with the release of our 1991 Estate Chardonnay in 1993. He and Ernest had just been photographed for the front cover of *Wine Spectator* magazine with a bottle of Estate Chardonnay in my grandfather's hand. The 1994 Estate Cabernet was released after his death. It was a difficult loss for us all, as he was paving the way for our fine wine initiatives. This picture was also included on the front cover of their book *Ernest & Julio—Our Story*.

Iconic photo of Ernest and my Grandfather Julio on the cover of Our Story, *published in 1994*

Working in the business at the time provided me opportunities for a lot of firsts, particularly in the growing premium category of our business where I was working. We were focused on introducing our fine wines, with special attention on the Gallo of Sonoma wines. Our winery facilities were expanding to include capabilities for this new direction, creating visitor experiences for trade and opening our first tasting room.

In the early 2000s, tasting rooms were becoming increasingly popular. In Sonoma County, vineyards and wineries are more dispersed, requiring guests to drive further, which is not always conducive to tasting wine. Since we were not open to the public and were mostly educating and entertaining our trade guests, press, and media, there was growing interest in exploring a tasting room for the consumer to experience our fine wines. So, I did.

The Gallo of Sonoma Tasting Room opened on Healdsburg Square in 2002. The guest experience was a sit-down, paid-for tasting accompanied by local artisan cheese and fresh local bread. The goal was to pair a quality experience with quality wines. Up until then, this type of tasting experience in Sonoma County was rarely done outside the vineyard and winery. It was a big risk, and we made the leap.

Subsequently, we opened our vineyards for tours, by appointment only, highlighting our wine-growing techniques and sustainable farming practices. I felt a sense of pride and accomplishment in providing our guests with a glimpse into our family, our history, our passion, and our fine wines. It was an exciting time and one I will never forget.

While my years in Sonoma were fulfilling and accomplished, I felt restless, and was yearning for more...

FOUR

The Tipping Point

In the year 2000, Malcolm Gladwell published his blockbuster book, *The Tipping Point*. In the introduction, Gladwell writes, "We need to prepare ourselves for the possibility that sometimes big changes follow from small events, and that sometimes these changes can happen very quickly." This book inspired the name of this chapter—it is where I found myself in 2005.

From the outside looking in, my life at the beginning of 2005 seemed ideal. I had given birth to three more beautiful children after returning to the United States and had settled into my many responsibilities at home and work. I was making a big impact in our family business, particularly in the fine wine category. I was focused in Sonoma and Napa, where we had acquired wineries like Louis M. Martini. I continued to work with Ernest, created the foundation of our Trade Hospitality and Communications departments, and I continued to build on the consumer experience in our tasting rooms. I also explored opportunities to open other tasting rooms and worked closely with brand managers on their marketing communications initiatives.

As lead spokesperson for our family, one of my favorite roles was hosting groups in Sonoma and Napa. I was honored to be representing and educating others about our family, our wines, and our legacy that two humble men created. I was giving them a sneak peek inside our family, conveying our commitment to quality and continuous improvement and leaving a lasting impression. This was gratifying and instilled a great sense of pride and appreciation for our history and heritage.

After eighteen years in the family business, I felt accomplished and was at the height of my career. I held many responsibilities, including managing a highly skilled team. I was responsible for cutting-edge initiatives and made valuable contributions to the growth of our fine wine brands. I was fully immersed in the work, and it consumed my time and energy.

Simply put, whether I realized it or not, my work had become my identity.

My husband and I enjoyed successful careers while expanding our family. I had a busy work and home life with four small children. We both traveled extensively for work, and I was commuting two hours a day. It was around this time that he had a pivotal career opportunity requiring him to live outside the country. The children were living with one foot in two countries, the United States and England, allowing them to be global citizens living, seeing, and experiencing life outside of what they had known. This was a significant change for our family and marriage. We were living apart and growing apart, and the situation was not sustainable. I found myself asking questions about our future.

My four children, Alexandra, Allison, Cameron, and Coleman

In reality, on the inside, my life was not ideal. I loved my career and loved my family, though the combination of it all was not working. It was too much. Something had to give.

How do you decide between the two—business first or family first?

I had to make changes, get back to basics, and concentrate on what mattered in life by shifting focus to my own family roots, putting me and my children first. I had lost my sense of purpose and my personal identity. These were confusing days that prompted me to examine all aspects of my life.

I started to wonder what my life would look like outside the shade of the family tree. This was a foreign concept, as I thought working in the business was a way of staying connected with family and my only career option. During the years in my career, I had not seen any family members leave the business, and I was confronted with a huge dilemma—If I leave the business, am I leaving the family? I was seeing more of my family on the job than off, so this question seemed like a reality, even though I knew deep down it was not true.

This would be a challenging step. I could hear family and friends say, "Why leave now?" I felt I could not share my thoughts and feelings as I knew they might talk me out of it and was worried they might succeed. So, I kept thoughts to myself. To make things even more difficult, Ernest was still alive and was enthusiastic about my involvement in the business. Every time I saw him, he asked, "How are things in Sonoma?" My quandary deepened.

The business was changing, evolving from its entrepreneurial roots to a professionally managed organization necessary for growth and expansion. The thought of leaving was difficult and making the final decision was even more so.

I was at a tipping point.

My Dilemma

I was facing a huge dilemma, one which I had never faced before. There were no role models for the place in which I found myself. Where could I go for answers? I needed to check in with myself, since what I was considering would change my life. I knew if I left the business, I would miss working closely with my family and those day-to-day business conversations, decisions, and initiatives I was leading. What would life be like outside the shade of the family tree? Who would I be? What would I do? I had more questions than answers.

In my contemplation, I reflected on an incident in 2002 at Vin Expo in Tokyo, Japan. In addition to representing our wines at one of the largest exhibitions for wine and spirit professionals from all over the world, I participated in a press conference with Japanese press and media. Until then, I had never experienced a press conference of this magnitude. It was held in the massive pavilion on the main stage, with spotlights all around and a flurry of media with cameras flashing. I was center stage. It felt intimidating. To add to it, there was a formality to the process where I was told in advance to pause after each complete thought for translation since no one spoke English, which caused the event to last twice as long.

I vividly recall a question, one that stumped me. This had rarely happened given my deep knowledge and expertise. A writer asked, "If you were not born into this family, what would you be doing now?" It was an intriguing question, one I had never been asked before. Probably for the first time, I thought about the possibility that there is life beyond the family business. I will never forget this question, as it was the start of my thinking that I could do something different.

The large crowd was waiting. I had to search quickly for an answer. With sweaty palms, I paused for what seemed like a long time and answered, "I would be a teacher." The reason why my response came so easily, even though it was forced in the moment, is because I had already been teaching naturally throughout my life. From a young age I took the opportunity to "teach" my younger siblings. I had a classroom set up with all the necessities—blackboard, chalk, teacher edition books, podium, and my three younger siblings as my students. My mom recalls how quiet things were in the next room as she was preparing dinner, and she realized I had all three intently listening to whatever I was teaching.

Education was at the core of my role in the family business. I was educating others about our company, wines, and vineyard properties all over the world, along with our history and anecdotal stories of my time with Ernest and my Grandfather Julio. I suppose this is where my own storytelling began. It all started in the vineyard when our customers, press, and media came to Sonoma and Napa to tour our vineyards and winery. Given my extensive knowledge, I often got asked whether I was a viticulturist or a winemaker. This was the greatest compliment I could receive.

The question—If I leave the business, am I leaving the family?—had been my dilemma. I thought the answer should be black or white, not knowing there was an unexplored gray area. With this spark, it shed new light on my decision—my unexplored gray area would soon become my focus and my new technicolor world.

To make that happen, I needed answers and a balanced view from someone not connected to our family business. I made the decision to engage with an executive coach to help me sort it all out and see a new perspective. Opening myself to an "outsider" felt uncomfortable, as revealing myself to others does not come naturally and causes me to feel vulnerable.

Over time I was able to trust the process and understand the reality of my intense situation. Deep in my heart I knew it was time for a change.

My Realizations

I came to realize my current work and family life situation was not sustainable. The fast pace of both and splitting my time between the two was starting to affect my health and well-being. There was a lot of change happening in the business, in my marriage, and with the growing needs of my four children. It was the perfect storm.

After much thought and reflection, I made two life-changing decisions—to leave the business and to leave my marriage. Both were the most difficult decisions in my life, deeply personal and painful, and ones not taken lightly. I did not have it all figured out. I knew if I stayed, I was comforting them, and if I left, I was comforting me. So, I took the time needed to understand and sort through the implications of these life-altering decisions before acting.

During this time, I found my *no*. I had spent a lot of time saying *yes* over the years when the real answer often should have been *no*. One of the lessons I learned working with Ernest about decision-making—"If you need an answer in this moment, the answer is *no*." I'll never forget that. I now respect the need to take time in making decisions.

I took the road less traveled. This could have been viewed as selfish. For me, it was self-care. I put my own oxygen mask on first, like on an airplane when you should put on your own oxygen mask before helping your child or anyone else. This life-giving mask gave me renewed strength and courage to make my way through these challenging decisions.

The Road not Taken

Two roads diverged in a yellow wood,
And sorry I could not travel both
And be one traveler, long I stood
And looked down one as far as I could
To where it bent in the undergrowth;

Then took the other, as just as fair,
And having perhaps the better claim,
Because it was grassy and wanted wear;
Though as for that the passing there
Had worn them really about the same,
And both that morning equally lay
In leaves no step had trodden black.
Oh, I kept the first for another day!
Yet knowing how way leads on to way,
I doubted if I should ever come back.

I shall be telling this with a sigh
Somewhere ages and ages hence:
Two roads diverged in a wood, and I—
I took the one less traveled by,
And that has made all the difference.

—Robert Frost, 1916

The two closing lines of Robert Frost's poem—*"Two roads diverged in a wood, and I took the one less traveled by, and that has made all the difference"*—summed up my decisions. I forged ahead to explore my unknown adventure.

FIVE

My Adventure Begins

"The call to adventure signifies that destiny has summoned the hero and transferred his spiritual center of gravity from within the pale of this society to a zone unknown. This fateful region of both treasure and danger may be variously represented: as a distant land, a forest, a kingdom underground, beneath the waves or above the sky, a secret island, lofty mountaintop, or profound dream state; but it is always a place of strangely fluid and polymorphous beings, unimaginable torments, superhuman deeds, and impossible delights."

—Joseph Campbell, The Hero with a Thousand Faces

Joseph Campbell's book, *The Hero with a Thousand Faces,* was published in 1949 and has had great influence on storytelling by recording artists, authors, poets, and Hollywood screenwriters. Filmmakers George Miller and George Lucas credit Campbell's work as inspiration for the mythic foundation of their epic series *Mad Max* and *Star Wars*. The genius of his work is that he combines modern psychology with his understanding of comparative mythology.

THE HERO'S
JOURNEY

The hero's journey is demonstrated in this common template involving a hero on a transformational adventure

Joseph Campbell outlines the hero's journey as the call to adventure, the road of trials, the vision quest, the meeting of the goddess, the boon, the magic flight, the return threshold, the master of two worlds. The journey is one of self-discovery, trials and tribulations of learning, wise and not-so-wise helpers, obtaining the elixir, and then returning "home."

While Campbell focused on the masculine perspective, Maureen Murdock published her book, *The Heroine's*

Journey, years later in 1990, based on Campbell's work and her interviews with him. This book shifts to include the feminine perspective and her journey.

I share all this as a foundation of the learning I gained on my great adventure of life. I realize my journey is not a new story. It is one that follows a pattern. Everyone's journey is different, though Campbell outlines some common themes. I made the journey around the "horn" and learned so much from so many people, places, and things that shape-shifted me.

Path to Personal Growth

There are many paths to the mount. There is no right or wrong path, and the trick in life is to find the one that works best for you. The fact is, we are all on a personal growth journey of some kind, whether we like it or not. In my experience, what we resist persists.

After making these two major decisions, a whole new world opened, and my adventure began. As I made my way forward, I did not look back, which was another insight I learned from Ernest. Once he made a decision it was done. He never looked back—he just made things better, improving upon the past. I felt there was something more waiting for me outside the shade of the family tree. I realized I inherited the entrepreneurial gene, and I knew I wanted to continue utilizing my leadership and business expertise in a way that worked for me and my family.

I was going through a lot of discovery, with no fixed plan in place. It is one thing to make a decision and it is another to take action. I knew it would be complicated. I started to explore the two worlds of my personal and professional life simultaneously and in a new way. It was uncharted territory.

This process was unsettling for my family, comforting for my children, and chaotic for me. Making the shift to working from home was a big transition. Even though it allowed me to be present for my children at a critical stage, it was a lifestyle to which I was not accustomed. I had always worked outside the home, and that is the only life we all knew. Unknowingly I recreated the chaos I was escaping as a child growing up in a busy household. By default, I had become a combination of my mother and father, the CEO and COO of the household.

During this time, I worked on how I could be a better person, mother, granddaughter, daughter, sister, and aunt. What does my future look like from here? My driving force was how I could be a more effective role model for my children and others.

To do this, I needed to be open to learning more about me, all parts, especially those I was unwilling or had no time to explore in my fast-paced life. I got curious, vulnerable, and sat with a lot of uncomfortable parts. I needed to find comfort in my discomfort, be authentic, and get aligned with myself.

My busy career did not lend itself to forming new friendships outside of work and family. Although my lifelong high-school and university friends are important to me, I was not connected with them much at that point. I was used to a fast-paced career life, though this stage of hustle and bustle was a new way of being. I was juggling four children, two households, two countries, two schools, children's activities and sports, and my professional and family life commitments. Life was overwhelming. I needed support and social connection.

I was reminded of Maslow's Hierarchy of Needs. I learned about his work growing up and was always fascinated by the stages of human growth. His pyramid is straightforward, easy to grasp, and used commonly today in psychology and business practices. It has always held great meaning for me and mapped my journey to self.

It reinforced my motivation for needs along the way. If my basic needs were not met, how could I be there for others? I needed to receive the basics before moving to the next level of achieving self-actualization. Unmet needs can affect the entire family.

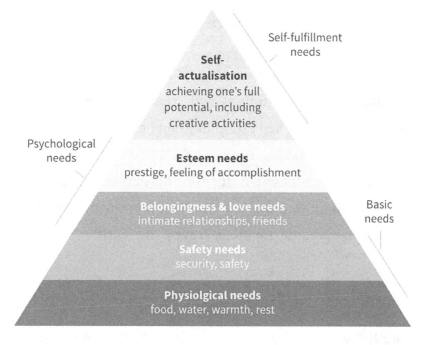

Maslow's Hierarchy of Needs, represented as a pyramid with basic needs at the bottom, then psychological needs followed by self-fulfillment needs at the top

In theory, this framework might look simple. In application, it was challenging in my stage of life at the time. To satisfy my psychological needs of belonging, for example, I needed social connection. In the past, my work had been my social life, and I needed to compensate for that in another way. So, I created new friendships in my community. Deep down I was looking for other women in similar situations and soon found them through parents of my children's friends and in the community. These women have become my dear friends.

One of those friends connected me with other women of interesting backgrounds and areas of expertise. They were an accomplished group of global businesswomen not accustomed to taking time out for self-care. This group, coined the "goddesses," focused on personal growth to balance their demanding careers, exploring exciting experiences and destinations around the world.

Journey of the Goddesses

In 2006 during a "goddesses" trip to France, a subset of the group decided to travel on to West Africa, where a friend of the group had been offered a job with Oxfam. It would be an adventure, and one that would change my life in many ways.

As usual, I was quite busy in the time before the trip, so my preparation and attention to detail was not ideal. I noticed emails requesting my bio and did not pay much attention at first. When the notices kept coming, I began to wonder why my bio was needed. Was it for entry into the country? For a visa? I was clueless. I was heading into unknown territory.

After arriving in Dakar, our first morning we were scheduled for a trip to Kédougou, south of Dakar, with the president of the local chamber of commerce as our host. He was excited to share his newly built compound and to show us some local businesses along the way, including his own marble quarry. That all sounded interesting, although driving ten hours each way was a small and important detail I missed on the itinerary. This trip was not for the faint of heart—in fact, not everyone in our group decided to go because of the lengthy travel involved and how much time it would take out of their pleasure trip.

For this long journey, we loaded up in three separate utility vehicles. I love road trips, and this one was for the record books as it was not quite what I expected. I set out as a tourist. At each stop I took pictures and continued to be fascinated by the new surroundings. As we got further into our trip, things changed—we encountered check points, and I was again wondering what we were getting into. The long haul included many "passage points," dangerous roadways with police and machine guns. We were swiftly allowed to pass thanks to our chamber of commerce host.

On the way, we met with several businesses looking for investment. We began contemplating how we could help in a greater way. We were a small group and did not know how we could have a major impact. We had many hours to work through the details, applying our diverse expertise from financial services and venture capital, to marketing and medical professionals. During our many stops, I could hear some of our group deliberating investment options and financial structures. I found myself focused on branding. I got inspiration from road signs and billboards, surveying fill-up stations and modest markets, while being curious about their culture. The long trip gave us plenty of time to brainstorm and get clear on the new investment project.

Hour after hour, I kept hearing our drivers and host speaking a language I did not understand, except the word *wow*. It was hypnotic to hear them repeatedly say throughout a conversation, "Wow, wow, wow, wow." After what seemed like an eternity in the back of those utility vehicles, I finally asked what *wow* meant. They told me it means *yes* in the local Wolof language. When I heard this definition, I thought, *That's it!* The perfect name for our investment group was WOW, also an acronym for "Women of the World," which we were. It was a positive outcome of our long journey to Kédougou.

After returning from our two-night long grueling trip away, we were back at our hotel in Dakar. The next morning, we met with one of the President of Senegal's ministers for breakfast. I now realized the need for our bios.

After breakfast we were whisked off to a community co-op (a community-based lending program for businesswomen) in Thiès, an hour north of Dakar that took twice as long due to congested traffic. Once at the community center, I noticed it was packed with hundreds of women, folders in hand, standing room only. I had no idea what I was getting into.

There was a formal table at the front with a crowd of press and media, a site with which I was familiar. Turns out, it was a press conference, and to my surprise we were the panelists. They introduced us and we answered questions from the press while the women watched and listened eagerly. After the press conference, we were divided by area of expertise and the women were given the opportunity to meet with us individually to ask questions and gain input on their business plans. We were there to give advice, and they were there seeking investments—this minor point was lost in translation. It soon became clear they needed both.

I recall the group of women I spoke with all had similar businesses—selling mangoes. Driving to the community center earlier I remember seeing, on both sides of the road, rows and rows of mangoes for sale—like mango malls. I did not see any differentiation between them other than the people who were selling them. While speaking with the group, I discovered they were operating separately even though they were selling the same product. I saw an opportunity for them to work together and thereby form a stronger business. I could see this was a foreign concept at first, and due to the language barrier, I gave them a visual. I picked up a stick and broke it, showing them what it looks like working by yourself. Then I picked up a bunch of sticks and tried to break them and could not, demonstrating they are stronger together than they are apart. I could see smiles and nods acknowledging they understood. This mirrored for me my grandmother's concept of family unity—we are stronger together—dramatically reinforced, even halfway across the world.

This was one of many women co-ops we met with during our trip. Each day became more intriguing and we were moved by their stories, hardships, and courage. These women were stepping up in their family and community to make their world a better place. What I witnessed first-hand was their hard work and dedication. They shared a close bond as a community with a common goal to make a difference and a shared responsibility for looking after each other. For example, they experienced each other's highs and lows and financial burdens. If one fell short, the rest were there for them. They were trustworthy and had a built-in honor system to repay their debt. This was amazing to me, as I had not experienced anything like it in modern society.

While in Thiès, our time was cut short as we received notice that the minister we met with that morning was so impressed with our group that the President of Senegal, Abdoulaye Wade, summoned us for an introduction. We quickly got in the vehicles for a long drive back for our private meeting with the President. Now that was a big deal.

After careful security clearance, we were led to a large room with a circular table where we sat with the President and his chiefs of staff. We discussed various topics, including experiences so far on our trip. We shared our idea of investing in women-owned businesses, and the President and his staff confirmed that the women were a much better investment than the men, who rarely paid their debts due to drinking and gambling. We discussed many other issues, including infrastructure, transportation, and the economy. It was a surreal and gratifying experience to be able to provide input directly to the President and his staff. Our knowledge and business expertise were welcomed and valued so much that his staff continued to stay in contact throughout our trip for additional feedback.

Meeting with the President of Senegal and his staff

Back at the hotel we continued our conversations about this budding investment project and how we could have impact in a meaningful way. A quote by Chinese philosopher Lao Tzu, founder of Taoism, says, "Give a man a fish, and you feed him for a day. Teach him how to fish, and you feed him for a lifetime." These were honest, hard-working women, dedicated to providing for their families in life-giving ways and they had proven track records of repaying their loans. Investing our time, talent, and resources in these women-owned businesses would be a rewarding endeavor to pursue.

The trip to Senegal that began as a pleasure trip turned out to be the most rewarding and satisfying business trip. It was a rigorous week, packed full of adventures. As a result of our efforts, we formed the social venture investment group WOW, an acronym for Women of the World. We raised and invested significant capital for a small group of women-owned businesses. At that time, non-government organizations (NGOs) were providing subsidies that were challenging the welfare of small, local businesses. Therefore, private sector involvement became more important to sustain local businesses. WOW offered investment, business expertise and on-the-ground support, currently not being offered by NGOs. WOW provided a successful business model solution. This caught the eye of Oxfam, a leading international organization focused on the alleviation of global poverty. They were looking to expand in the private sector, and having a connection with our friend there helped. Since day-to-day management was not an option for us given our careers, we partnered together and then eventually turned operations over to Oxfam.

With two women in Dakar, Senegal, discussing investments

One of our founders was invited to present at the prestigious Clinton Initiative, founded in 2005 and known for impact investing in the world. A few years later, we had the opportunity to speak at the newly formed Social Capital Markets (SOCAP) Conference in San Francisco. A short documentary was also made showcasing the businesses in which we invested. Social impact investing aligned well with my entrepreneurial skills, as it was a concept on the leading edge. We were ahead of our time.

To the Depths and Back

This investment venture required significant effort and travel. I had many travels to Senegal over the years, and on one trip in 2006, something happened that would change my life.

This last-minute trip was to conduct due diligence on prospective businesses for investment. It was a long day, as most of the businesses were located in the outskirts of Dakar. Dreaded transportation out of the city took twice as long due to lack of infrastructure. Most of the roads were unpaved, and those that were paved were very rough. The roads were filled with traffic—all types of vehicles jammed together trying to push their way out of the city. It took well more than an hour just to reach the city limits and at least another hour or so to reach our destination just north of Dakar in the middle of nowhere.

On one of our stops, we walked the property, which was blazing hot with mosquitos galore. The layout looked similar to many of our winery facilities, so I surmised it was some kind of food processing facility—and it was. It turned out to be an abandoned juice processing plant. During the visit, I could see the potential because I had seen facilities like this in action and knew this was a diamond in the rough. The surroundings were bare, and location was a challenge due to transportation restrictions. I imagine this is what it must have looked like in the early days of California before there was commercial development. Ironically, there was an old inoperative train track in place leading straight through the plant. This was an awe-inspiring moment as it was similar to the epicenter of our winery beginnings in Modesto. It was a nostalgic day, highlighting a time when my Grandfather Julio visited co-operative winery facilities and was breaking new ground in search of expanding winemaking capabilities.

This particular trip brought great satisfaction on many levels, including feeding my entrepreneurial spirit. I found the entire Africa project rewarding, as it strengthened my ability to mentor individuals and families interested in these endeavors. It was a grassroots effort with real, on-the-ground experience.

When I returned to California, I started to feel sick. My symptoms were mild at first. I felt lightheaded, dehydrated, and got progressively worse every day with flu-like symptoms. I remember my children were home from England for the summer. I tried to occupy them until the next morning when my sister Joan and her husband arrived to take me to the emergency room. I continued to spiral, never feeling this much pain before, not even in childbirth. In the hospital, they did not know what it was. When they learned I had been to Africa, they took a blood test and concluded I had malaria—not just any kind—the most lethal kind, falciparum malaria.

In the San Francisco Bay Area, contracting malaria was unheard of. To treat this strain, an infectious disease doctor had to prescribe quinine, a powerful drug to kill the parasite and prevent it from growing. Since it was not readily available, I was being held in the emergency room until they could reach one of three infectious disease doctors in the county. They tried to contact them repeatedly, as they were not on call nor in demand. It seemed like an eternity waiting for the authorization of quinine to be transferred from the UCSF hospital just across the bay.

I was in much pain and getting worse. I kept asking the on-call doctor when the medication would arrive and the response was, "Bad news/good news—once you take the medication you are going to feel worse before you get better." It sounded counter-intuitive. I had no idea the magnitude of what that meant until later.

When they received confirmation that the quinine was in transit, they were able to assign me to a hospital room.

Once there, a series of doctors rotated through over a short period of time and kept asking the same questions over and over. I finally got so perturbed and asked with irritation, "Why are you asking me the same questions?" There was no response. Later I would find out that they were trying to keep my mind active as a precaution, since this type of malaria affects the brain.

Just as I was starting to get settled into the room, an orderly wheeled in a large gurney and said, "We need to move you to the intensive care unit." This happened so abruptly, with no explanation. An ICU unit? Why? That sounded serious. I think my sister gasped and was trying to hold back tears to stay strong for me. I was feeling restless from the pain and surrendered to everything going on around me. I laid down on the gurney and on the way to ICU, I asked, "Am I going to die?"

The orderly wheeling the gurney responded, "I don't know."

My sister Joan was the only member of my family who was there with me. She later shared that she felt helpless and was hiding her tears most of the time. When she called my parents, I do not think they fully grasped how grave my illness was. After all, it was unfathomable to think I could die from this thing called malaria. My sister lived the closest, so she was "in charge." I think this must have been terrifying for her. She was my strength and has always been there for me. In fact, she was like a second mother. When asked about my growing-up years, my mom always said, "Caroline was easy to raise." and my sister would responded, "What do you mean? I was the one who raised her!"

While in the hospital, I had no knowledge of all that was going on behind the scenes and was only told later. I was in the ICU for more than a week. It was necessary to be monitored closely while the quinine was administered, as it could have adverse effects such as heart and lung failure. I experienced both. To add to that, the deadly parasite was aggressively attacking my red blood cells, causing rapid weakness in my body. I finally understood what the ER doctor meant when told I was going to feel worse before getting better.

After leaving ICU, they moved me to a hospital room again. After weeks of constantly drawing blood from me, they ran out of places to draw from, eventually moving to my ankles. They said it was necessary to collect samples each day—enough to send to the county and state for analysis, as they had never seen a live case of this type of malaria. After so much time, I told them jokingly, "You have taken so much blood from me, I would like a sample to take home as a symbol of my war wound."

They said, "We do not do that."

I replied in jest, "I am sure you can find a way."

Sure enough, when I was finally allowed to leave the hospital, the staff surprised me. They wheeled me out of the hospital via the lab. When we entered the lab, the entire staff gave me a standing ovation, clapping loudly, excited to meet "the malaria patient." One of the lab attendants enthusiastically said that the only time they had seen a case like mine was in a textbook. They proceeded to put a glass slide under the microscope and moved my wheelchair in front of it, helping me stand as they invited me to take a look. It was the malaria that had taken over my body so quickly. They removed the slide and one of the staff members said, handing me the glass slide in a safe case, "Here, this is yours. You deserve this—it will be a great reminder of your triumph over this deadly strain of malaria." I occasionally look at it as a reminder of how grateful I am to be alive.

After recovering from my illness, I "got back on the horse" and traveled back to Africa several times, always certain to take my anti-malaria medication. I often wonder what life is like there now. I am sure there has been much progress since then, and I hope to return someday.

My Road Ahead

Once home from the hospital, it was a long recovery process on all levels. I had to pace my activity, since simple movements were taxing to my heart and lungs. I had to learn to breathe again, as my lungs were greatly affected. It was a lengthy process just to move around the room, and that was my "exercise."

It was during my recovery period that I learned about the power of life, setback, and triumph, a small taste of what my Grandfather Alfred must have experienced with his sticks. My friendships and local community rallied together to take care of many of my needs, including meals, during this difficult time. I did not know the extent of all the efforts until much later. After I was improving and getting around more by myself, my youngest son asked me, "Mom, how come there are no meals on the doorstep?" I was grateful for all the support, love, and kindness that were demonstrated. It was a reminder of the importance that friendship and community provide in good times and in bad, and this was one of those times.

How do you come back from a near-death experience? This was a rare and deadly form of malaria. I was told by my doctor in a follow-up appointment that those who survive it never get it again. I realized the gravity of the situation and how fortunate I was to survive. I took this time to get connected with myself, reflecting on what brought me great joy and passion. My purpose in life became even more important to me. I decided to live each day as if it were my last, because it very well could be. I had no appreciation for that statement up until my experience with malaria. While some might see a near death as an ending—for me it was a beginning.

The 1994 movie *Shawshank Redemption* tells the story of a banker, played by Tim Robbins, who is serving a life sentence despite his claims of innocence. Over the decades of imprisonment, he befriends a fellow prisoner, played by Morgan Freeman, and they become close friends. When Robbins's character shares his dream outside of prison, he delivers the famous line, "It comes down to a simple choice—get busy living or get busy dying."

The choice was mine. I got busy living.

My Adventure Continues

My travels to Africa were just the start of my personal adventure. I had a second chance at life. I continued my exploration in the personal growth world. My motivation was to learn all I could, as I had done in the business world. I also had a new reason to discover all aspects of myself and what I aspired to be. I had a lot of people depending on me, especially my children, and getting in touch with the best version of myself was the most valuable gift I could give them. I got curious and was hungry for more.

I discovered a lot of modalities, and although some had a huge impact on my personal growth, I realized they were not all for me. My first discovery was the world of coaching, a growing field misunderstood by many at the time. I found my own experience with an executive coach to be extremely positive and quite useful during my tipping point. I knew I would benefit from the process, so I made the decision to get certified as an executive coach, regardless of whether or not I pursued it professionally. My coaching cohort represented a diverse group of traditional executives looking for a change or transition in their business careers. They were people from a variety of commercial industries, from healthcare to tax and financial to legal backgrounds, all accomplished in their areas of expertise.

I went on to discover many other non-traditional methods and certifications in areas such as Neuro-Linguistic Programming (NLP), Conscious Language, The School for the Work of Byron Katie, and Council Training, to name a few. I was a ferocious learner and a sponge for knowledge, participating in a plethora of workshops. So, when a friend suggested a workshop called the Radically Alive Leader, it added to my growing list of workshops. The work was body-based and resonated with me on a deeper level— so much so that I sought out more. Eventually it led me to enroll in the Radical Aliveness Institute, an intensive four-year training program that proved to be life-changing. I thought I had gone deep in my first workshop and only after graduation realized I was just scratching the surface. I could see benefit for myself and application for families, especially those in business together.

I was immersed with a cohort and we bore intense witness to each other over the course of four years. It was challenging and rewarding at the same time. This type of work is multi-faceted and was healing for me on many levels. The professional practitioner certification program consisted of five residential training modules per year in Los Angeles with four days of classes during each module. I remember fellow students at the school went home feeling exhausted. For me, I had another "group" waiting at home—my four children, challenging me at every turn, while constantly inspiring me to be a better parent.

In my work with families, especially of multi-generational construct, it has been an invaluable resource to effectively manage family dynamics, ensuring every voice is heard, and to guide productive conservations.

Radical Aliveness Institute has become a leading-edge global movement and continues to evolve, addressing broader issues facing our world today. I was in the third graduating class and went on to be a founding board member of the Institute.

Vision Quests

In addition to my inner work, my travels fed the adventurer in me and fueled my desire to further explore the world. In parallel to my personal journey, I began to research what other families do when confronted with a similar dilemma. Like my personal growth journey and anything I do in life, I took it on with intense focus and purpose. I discovered the world of family business, a new world of undiscovered resources, and in the beginning it was overwhelming. To my surprise and delight, I found an entire industry dedicated to family businesses. Like in the wine industry, there were dedicated trade and membership associations, academic institutions, and professionals. Historically the wine business had been predominately family-owned and-operated businesses, and because of this, my discovery of the family business world seemed like a natural progression.

The education process of my personal growth and family business industry kept me intellectually stimulated, and I unexpectantly found commonality that traversed both psychology and business. I was hooked, and I recall personal growth and family business books becoming my "pleasure reading." That remains true today.

I also attended family business conferences, events, and workshops in the United States and Europe. The more I learned, the more I realized families are simply families with different last names, cultures, and backgrounds. Though they have different stories, they face similar issues.

The scientist in me recognized recurring themes and analyzed the research and common practices of family businesses and how to apply all I learned to my family. I shared the information with my family and initiated our family governance and beyond.

I found immediate connections and opportunities for involvement through attending these events. Learning from other families coupled with what I knew from my own family experience gave me a good reason to participate on panel discussions, in speaking engagements, and in keynotes. In addition to networking with other families and professionals, I was pleasantly surprised when it took me around the world. I had finally combined two of my passions for family business and travel. It was an organic process and the start of forming my own business—Premier Growth—eventually working with other families.

I was invited to speak with a business colleague at a Family Business Network (FBN) Asia conference in Malaysia. Even though the culture and language were very different, the family issues and concerns were similar. There was much passion for family and keen interest in learning in new and different ways. The FBN leadership added to the enthusiasm, and it was contagious. Given this positive experience, I was introduced to the local FBN lead contact in the United States, who was establishing their board governance for a domestic chapter. I was then recruited to serve on their task force to achieve this objective and went on to serve as a board member. I also served on their international committee for sustainability. Over the course of my ten-year involvement with FBN, I experienced many different roles, meeting dynamic families and visiting interesting places around the globe, including Spain, England, Switzerland, Singapore, Malaysia, Indonesia, China, and the Philippines.

I found this travel quite different and rewarding, as I was visiting countries with members of other like-minded family businesses. These experiences, called "learning journeys," were hosted by local families. We got an insider look through their eyes into their city, culture, and businesses. It felt natural and was like home away from home. This created a new way of travel for me, taking in my surroundings while connecting with fellow family participants. I got into the habit of arriving at my destination early enough to have time to experience the culture.

This concept of going into a country earlier was not only sparked by the learning journeys with FBN—it also reminded me of a business trip I had taken to the Netherlands while working in our family business. I had usually traveled in and out of a location without taking extra time to explore it. On this particular trip, I learned how taking time, even briefly, would serve me.

After a long international flight, I checked in at the hotel in the afternoon. Wanting to stay awake and get acclimated to the local time zone in preparation for a full day of meetings the next day, I decided to walk. I inquired about local points of interests, grabbed a map, and was off. I was most intrigued by two museums, especially since they were conveniently located a five-minute walk apart—The Rijksmuseum and the Van Gogh Museum. I knew I had a good chance of seeing both before closing time, a lofty goal given I had only a few hours. A speed-walking visit was my approach, and after being cooped up on an airplane for so long, it was a welcomed activity, especially since I was pregnant.

The next morning, I met with one of the most prestigious wine writers in the country. He had some preconceived notions of America and even more so about our wines. I knew this meeting would be challenging and was prepared, although not prepared for his first question. He asked, "What do you know of our country?" Given my arrival the previous day, I had answers, many of which I discovered while walking the streets, interacting with locals, and visiting the two museums. Apparently that was not easy to do, as he was surprised. He also challenged my wine knowledge, assuming that I knew only about California wines. Having recently traveled to Bordeaux on a research trip exploring first-growth wines, and having lived and worked internationally, I was able to draw on my global experience and expertise. He told me he was impressed. I was honored, as he did not give compliments freely. His view of me, and our wines changed, and he thanked me for opening his eyes.

This new way of travel became my new routine. I arrived early and lingered after, not only to adjust and acclimate myself to the time zone, also to take in my surroundings and experience the land, the people, and the culture. I found this served me in business and also fulfilled a personal interest. This was the start of my two worlds blending together.

This was demonstrated on one of my first trips to Australia and New Zealand.

My sister Anne and her family were planning an around-the-world adventure, and I wanted to meet up with them during their travels. I asked where they would be the longest, and she said Australia and New Zealand. I had always wanted to travel there. The stars aligned, and I was leaving on a two-week trip that turned into eight.

With my sister Anne and her family in Christchurch, New Zealand

Before leaving, I asked a family business colleague for suggestions of business contacts, and I connected with them throughout my trip, receiving local input and valuable opinions of places to visit. I zig-zagged my way, part of the time with family and part of the time on my own. My adventures were off the beaten path and not in a guidebook, and I have plentiful stories to fill an adventure book someday.

In Australia and New Zealand, I met with local families, their businesses, and family office leadership. I also met with two membership organizations—Private Wealth Network (PWN) and Family Business Australia (FBA).

While in Marlborough, New Zealand, I learned to drive on the on the "wrong" side of the road—quite the experience at first. It soon became natural. I also visited one of our winery partners, Whitehaven.

Driving on the "wrong side" of the road in New Zealand

On this particular trip, I was moved by the vastness of the land and at times felt like I was the only person on earth. It gave me a sense of freedom and newfound spiritual connection to the land, nature, and its people. The feelings were massive and overwhelming. My experience there is one I cannot put into words and was beyond imagination. As they say in Australia, I went on a "walkabout." The land guided me to places undiscovered and unplanned, transporting me to a dreamlike place.

I recently read the book *Songlines*. It was written by Bruce Chapman, who was interested in the "navigational tracks" that weave across the country of Australia and are thought to be a map of ancient wisdom of aboriginal culture. The elders trained their people to "sing the landscape" while moving from location to location. Their history is preserved and passed down through song, dance, art, and stories of the "dreamtime." This book rekindled my experience and reminded me of the peace and tranquility I found there.

Exploring Uluru-Kata Tjuta National Park in Australia at sunset

This transformative quest, along with making meaningful business contacts, were reason enough to return a month later for a five-city speaking engagement. This fruitful business trip has led to lasting business relationships and the global expansion of my business.

Over time, my business and travel found rhythm and synchronicity. An example is on my extreme quest to Bhutan. A family business colleague connected me with an organization for business synergies. Next thing I knew, I was packing for Bhutan. It is located in the eastern Himalayas and is known for its Gross National Happiness (GNH)—no joke. The Kingdom of Bhutan is currently ruled by a young king, forty years old, and their democracy is grounded in their national values, stemming from their constitution based on Buddhist philosophy. The Gross National Happiness Initiative, conducted every five years, measures nine key areas of happiness—psychological well-being, health, education, good governance, ecology, time use, community vitality, culture, and living standards. If a policy or development does not pass through the filter of the happiness index, it is not approved. Their strong values-based system, putting national interest before personal interest, intrigued me, as it correlated with the culture of a family.

With the Himalayas as a backdrop, this executive education trip was led by a team of educators relaying the intersection of business innovation and contentment. Fellow participants were professionals around the globe. This was a career highlight as experiential hands-on learning events had become part of my professional offering for family businesses.

Our journey was principally focused on contentment, the hallmark of the country. The meaning was demonstrated by locals and our guides, especially on those long, grueling treks to the "heavens." Because of the altitude, at times I felt I could not make the rigorous climb. Thanks to my guide who selflessly assisted and encouragement from my fellow participants, I succeeded and made it to the top of each climb. This is so true in life. Just when we think we cannot go any farther or ascend any higher, there is usually someone willing to lend a hand, and I had many.

We visited the famous Tiger's Nest and other not-as-famous monasteries. We were given an insider's look into one, where we received a special long-life blessing—a rare ceremony with monks and a Rinpoche, known in Tibetan Buddhism as a highly respected religious teacher. I even got to experience archery, the national and most popular sport in Bhutan, reminding me of my Grandfather Alfred.

Even though I did not use his "tripod" stance, after repeated practice and trial and error, I hit the target.

Receiving a special long-life blessing

Archery in Bhutan

Usually a trip of this magnitude would be well-thought-out and planned far in advance. To be honest, if that was the case, it probably would not have happened, since it was not on my bucket list. I embraced the opportunity, as it lined up with my schedule as if it were meant to be. I love it when things fall into place effortlessly, because it gives me a big YES to proceed. Going forward, this was the inner guidance I relied on when at a crossroads.

Departing Bhutan

It is impossible to convey the intense impact of all my personal and professional growth journeys. Wisdom comes from many people and places and is at the core of my life experiences. The culmination of all my adventures emphasized the value of life, the worth of living and breathing in the moment, and the importance of being rooted in family.

SIX

Start Where You Are and Grow as You Go

"Congratulations! Today is your day. You're off to Great Places! You're off and away!"

—*Dr. Seuss*

I have been a lifelong fan of Dr. Seuss books. I grew up with them and as a mother I read his books repeatedly with my own children, continuing the tradition of sharing his wisdom. This chapter is named for a mantra I created and use often that was inspired by his book, *Oh, the Places You'll Go!* It was first published in 1990, and was the last book published in his lifetime. The book is about the journey of life and its challenges. It is my inspiration for "start where you are and grow as you go," meaning start with what is in your sphere of influence and grow from there.

Where to Start?

My family gave me purpose through my experiences of being born, growing up, working, and now finding a new way to contribute. My motivation was to give back in a meaningful way and bridge the generations while instilling the values and vision of our founders. I found all paths led back to family.

I recognized it would be a herculean task. Was I up for the challenge? It was time to act and apply all I learned. It would be a long-term commitment and one I was willing to undertake to ensure our family legacy is sustained for generations to come—a grow-as-you-go process.

After my near-death experience, I continued to immerse myself in both the personal growth and family business worlds. I also continued my board roles, including my term on the board of directors of our family business and Sonoma State Wine Business Institute, where I am founding board president and have served since 2002.

However, I channeled my skills and expertise in a new way.

After listening and learning from other families and professionals, I was excited to share what I was learning with my family, and soon realized they did not understand or see a need. I get it—after, all we had a strong business and a strong family.

In meeting with families, I heard inspirational stories of those who endured for many generations and others who did not make it past the third generation. I observed strong businesses with family members who did not get along nor had interest in working for the family business. On the flip side, I experienced strong families with weak businesses. We had both a strong business and strong family. We had the perfect ingredients. What would we need to do to keep it that way?

What I learned is that most family businesses fail after the third generation. There are many proverbs throughout the world that suggest this theme. In the United States and United Kingdom, the saying is "shirtsleeves to shirtsleeves in three generations." In Japan, the expression goes, "Rice paddies to rice paddies in three generations." The Scots say, "The father buys, the son builds, the grandchild sells, and his son begs." In China, the proverb is "Wealth never survives three generations."

I did not want to be one of the families that did not continue to thrive.

I was starting to see significant change in our family—we were growing in numbers and becoming more geographically dispersed. In my generation, the third generation, family members were getting married, having children, and some were getting divorced. My experience growing up was all family members getting together for holidays and special events in one location. As the family grew, branches of the family were starting to have their holidays and events at their in-laws, splintering into smaller gatherings.

Growing up, my generation—the third, or G3—was fully immersed in our family values and culture. The first and second generation were successful at instilling strong values by living them. The question looming was how will the younger generation stay connected to founders they never met? What if we started to take the strength of family unity for granted? What would be the consequences?

I reflected on how I could share my learning and convince my family change was needed.

Given that our family was growing with more and more family members not working in the business, I decided to take a business approach to organizing our family.

Family Governance

Governance was a foreign topic for our family. It was originally introduced by a family advisor. This concept was most difficult in the beginning as it did not register with the family, especially now with a majority not working in the business. They had a business relationship to governance, not a family one. For them, there was not a need to put structure around something as obvious as family. Our advisor was a great support during this initial step to adopt and implement family governance.

What about those family members not working in the business? Did they have a say, and were they allowed to give input? If so, in what areas?

I discovered not all family members need or want to work in the family business. There are different options for engagement. I was introduced to the three-circle model of the family business system developed at Harvard Business School by Renato Tagiuri and John Davis. The three-circle model is comprised of three spheres—ownership, family, and business. To an outsider looking in, this model may look simple. For more than forty years, academics, business families, and their advisors have been sketching these three circles to gain insight into the inner workings of their family business and family business relationships. From my own experience, it is no simple task.

While officially working in the business, I was in the epicenter of all three circles. In other words, I was a family member, an owner, and in business management. Being in one circle is less complex, though navigating all three circles gets complicated. Once I understood this model in further detail, I realized there were options I never considered. I could be a family member and an owner, and not work in the business. This revelation opened my eyes to a new way of contributing to my family.

THREE-CIRCLE MODEL
OF THE FAMILY BUSINESS SYSTEM

OWNERSHIP

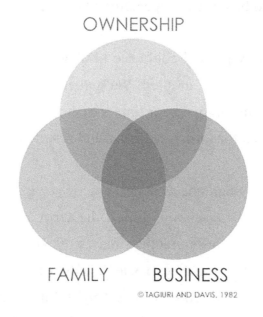

FAMILY   BUSINESS

© TAGIURI AND DAVIS, 1982

The Three-Circle Model showing three interdependent and overlapping groups—family, ownership, and business

I understood from my research that this area of family governance is a long-term process—just like planting vineyards and olive trees. I learned early on that you plant grapes for your children and olive trees for your children's children. Grapes and olive trees take a long time to grow and produce quality fruit. This is the "law of the farm," one I grew up with, and it means you cannot rush the farm. It takes three to five years before yielding the first quality harvest of grapes. For olives, it typically takes much longer—sometimes twelve years, depending on the variety, and up to sixty-five years to reach maximum yield. I learned to be patient, especially when it comes to family.

As the family grew, I could see how we could eventually take our family for granted. We gathered at holidays and special events, enjoyed our time together and got along, so why the need for formal structure and scheduled meetings?

My research taught me what best practices were the industry standards. I have always found the term *best practices* tricky, because those practices may work for some though not for all. The practices I was discovering were around forming a family council, creating a formal governing document, and conducting formal family meetings. I knew the formality of it all would not work for our family. There was definitely a need for formal structure in the business, though I was not sure they could see it for our growing family. I understood the "what" to do. The key was "how" to do it. This seemed like an impossible task. Would they be ready? It is all about time and timing and where and how to start.

My criteria were to keep it simple, find the right fit for our family, and make it easy to understand and implement. Otherwise, it would not happen.

If I wanted our family to adopt these common practices, I would need to be the one to step up and introduce them. I knew my family. I knew our business. So how could I put the two together? I needed to strategize the best way to introduce and implement these concepts.

I grew up as an observer with years of practice "learning" my family. Growing up in a family with eight children, a fraction of the size of our greater family, and working in the family business, things can get complicated. My survival techniques were using common sense, relying on resourcefulness, keeping things simple, being patient, and finding solutions.

On the business side, where I officially worked for eighteen years (and unofficially since birth), I learned the complexities of a family business. I worked during a time of expansion that required an entrepreneurial skill set. I strengthened my leadership and problem-solving skills, resilience, determination, creativity, and efficiency.

Bridging my keen sense of family and business dynamics proved to be the link needed to be a successful catalyst and initiate our family governance. Beyond structure, there was the need for engagement, education, communication, and organized activities such as meetings and events outside of holiday and business functions. Also, how will the younger generation gain knowledge about our business, especially if they choose to not work in the company? How are we going to nurture the family unity that my grandmother had instilled in us?

The other question keeping me up at night was, *why do this*? In fact, many family members asked me that very question, and the only thing I could find myself saying was, "Because it's the right thing to do." For me, the purpose was to strengthen our family legacy, supporting both the family and the business for future generations.

Now to convince them.

First Steps

It was time to put my sales skills to the test. I was making a recommendation to the family, not the business. I knew for those working in the business, data and metrics were important for decision-making. How could I bring data to something that is historically not data-driven? How could I communicate it in a way that everyone could understand? Using my criteria, I needed to keep it simple, find the right fit for our family, and make it easy to understand and implement.

During my research, I found an industry assessment tool being used to help families in areas of family and business governance. I eventually partnered with the original researcher and developer of the tool and we transformed it to an online version that is currently offered through my business today, called FEAT—Family Enterprise Assessment Tool. It gathers perceptions and feedback on family and business dynamics, providing useful data in a concise format. What I liked about this tool is it not only provided metrics, it also provided anonymity so that every voice could be heard.

For our family, the issue was more about what family members were not saying versus what they were saying. Opinions matter, and it is important to feel heard regardless of whether the feedback is used. It promotes open communication, transparency, and respect. How can we get feedback from everyone, especially those who do not speak up?

In order to get maximum participation, I started with my sphere of influence—my own generation, G3. I had always been close to my siblings and cousins, so it was a natural starting point. I introduced the idea of taking the assessment and received a 100 percent participation rate.

In a family, everyone can interpret things differently. I might feel one thing based on my life experiences, while other family members might feel another way, based on theirs. Being one of eight children, we all had different experiences growing up in our family, based on our age, birth rank, gender, and memories. One can imagine how these details have impact in large families.

For example, my oldest sibling, my youngest sibling, and I, right in the middle, grew up with very different perspectives and outlooks on life.

In getting feedback, there are no right or wrong answers, it is just the way one feels about something and his or her experience. It made me flash back to my days meeting with wine writers, each with their own opinion and description of the same wine. The framework to describe an experience with wine is based on sight, smell, taste, touch, and overall impression. Each wine writer had his or her own perception based on their experience with the wine. When asked which wine I liked best, I commonly answered, "It is like choosing between my children. I love them all, they each have their own special qualities, and I enjoy them in different ways and occasions, so how can I choose between them? They are all my favorite!"

The assessment of our family revealed varying perceptions. I used the data, paired with my learnings and common practices in the family business world, and made a formal pitch to my generation at the end of one of our business meetings. In my presentation, I gave an overview of the family business landscape, including resources and what other like-minded families were doing. I shared our assessment results and gave my recommendation, including forming a family council. I then outlined next steps and asked, "What do you want to do?"

There was a unanimous vote to proceed with the recommendation, and the next thing I knew I was voted in as chair of our family council. This was the beginning of our path to family governance and what I call "start where you are and grow as you go."

Off and Away

To start, our family council structure was composed of a representative from each family branch. The intention of the council was for family members to provide feedback in a constructive and democratic way. It was also to encourage engagement in activities, communication, and education. I created an acronym to describe this—ACE—as I am an avid card player and knew these were areas to ace for our family.

Initially there was confusion, and many did not understand the role of a family council. It sounded formal, and the difference between the family council and our board of directors was not clear. Some of the family council members were also on the board of directors, and that added to the confusion. There was concern that the family council could somehow compete with or repeat the board's agenda. It was an unfamiliar concept not understood at that time. It represented a change, and change is often challenging.

We had some major questions. What are the agenda items for the family council? What does the family council actually do? And finally, how will the family council measure results? They were very business-like questions to this newly formed, undefined group, and the family was looking to me for answers.

To come up with the answers, I used a combination of my business expertise along with my family business insight. I started with a charter, a lean document defining our roles, goals, and purpose that helped clarify the family council. It included a graphic to visually show the interaction of the family, council, and board. This was the most formal document created and served to convey clarity and purpose.

We set out to define our family values, culture, vision, and mission, soon realizing our values are closely tied to our founders and the family business. During this time, the greater family was expanding with the introduction of in-laws, and each family was adopting their own set of values. Given the growing family and diversity of our values, we decided to honor the family values of our founders. From that point it was clear we were not going to sit in a room and define our culture or values. It was clear that we were going to live them. So that is what we did.

We then created the following unity statement:

In order to remain a family-owned business for generations to come, we will foster family unity and connection to our heritage by living our culture and values through family traditions, communication, and education.

The Fun Side

Instead of a formal approach, we went to the other extreme—the fun side. After putting together and getting approval for our family council charter and unity statement, I decided to focus on engagement by creating fun events to get family members together outside of business and holidays.

I started with a grassroots approach. Since we are a wine family, it seemed only natural to make wine together. It would be fun, educational, and a sustainable project requiring us to get together several times throughout the year.

Our first event was held in our Founder's Vineyard, followed by a good old-fashioned barbecue dinner at my cousin Tom and his wife's home, formerly the home of my grandparents, Julio and Aileen. Tom was an early supporter of the family council, and his enthusiasm made a big difference in our success. The event was reminiscent of our roots, picking grapes in the vineyard while the children stomped them ala *I Love Lucy* style in her famous television episode stomping grapes in Italy. That was our first crush from our Founder's Vineyard, named for Ernest and Julio. What I found most interesting is that our target was G3 family members—and unexpectedly, the second generation,

G2, showed up to check it out, thinking we were having a meeting without them. Unknown to us at the time, we were creating attraction-based activities.

Me and my cousin Tom
at our first harvest event

Picking grapes at Founder's Vineyard

Stomping grapes ala "Lucy" style

Our next event was a label-naming gathering for our generation's winemaking project. It was our first year, and we needed a name for the label, so we created a contest. Although it was open to everyone, it was the fourth generation, G4, who submitted almost all of the entries. The winning name was First Crush, since you can only have one "first crush." From then on it was Second Crush, Third Crush, Fourth Crush, and now we are up to our Tenth Crush. It was a name that started organically and continues today.

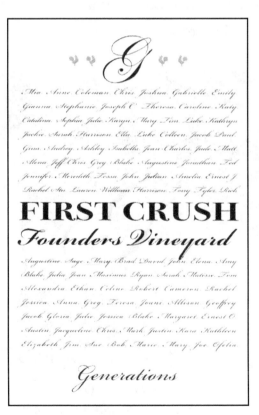

Our "First Crush, Generations" wine label

For this event, we also started a tradition of education for our children to learn experientially through activities with materials made from our businesses. The idea was sparked by the teacher in me and included creating labels and filling bottles with either sand or fun things like candy. It gave them an understanding of what we do and the products we make. Then the children were invited to share their label design adhered to their filled bottle. For some, it was their first public speaking engagement. It was adorable, and my children still have their bottles as a keepsake. That was the beginning, and it grew from there. Grow as you go!

Our label-naming event for our generation's winemaking project

My son Cameron with his finished product

We had our wine and we had our name. Now we needed to bottle it. Given that we had all the material and equipment needed, our next event was easy to execute. This was a roll-up-your- sleeves and get-your-hands-dirty event. Our generation and our families joined in and got busy choosing their different roles from filling the bottles, hand-corking, putting on labels by hand, and packing the bottles into cases. This was the final step of making our first wine together. Everyone was focused intently and the generations were engaging with each other, demonstrating teamwork. And oh, by the way, we were all having fun!

Separately, curiosity was building from the G2. They heard we were having events and they were not invited—maybe this intrigued them even more. More and more G2 continued to show up, especially after the first two events as word was getting out. I think they must have wondered what was so top-secret. They were showing up only to find us on an assembly line where everyone was working hard, creating a new tradition of making wine together and having fun in the process.

With my dad and son Coleman at one of our bottling events

With my daughter Allison in the barrel cellar

Like our events, the family council meetings evolved over time. Initially, they were held at the conclusion of a business meeting. The council and I decided it was time for a change so we could separate our council activities from these formal business meetings. I got the idea of utilizing our many beautiful properties to get us back to our family roots.

At one particular meeting, I stood up and said, "Let's get back to our family roots. Next year we're camping out, so bring your tents." I remember the family looked at me like I was crazy, and I said, "Yes, we're camping out, it's all part of the bonding experience." So, the next year we camped out, and it has become a tradition.

Family arriving at the campout

I created a format to honor the G2 women and their talents, finding a way that they could contribute to these events, such as sharing family archive photos and recipes (including a ravioli demonstration), organizing a spiritual service, and showcasing family talent. The weekend started Friday afternoon with all families setting up their camp. We then enjoyed a barbeque and an outdoor movie. The next morning, we had a camp breakfast followed by traditional family sports like volleyball, archery, football, corn-holing and kids' arts and crafts. We bottled wine together, took a group picture that became an annual tradition, ate lunch, and had a variety of afternoon activities intended to mix up the generations and get them interacting with each other. Sunday was morning breakfast after which we packed up camp and went our various ways.

My daughter Alexandra and son Cameron learning archery

We were living out our values and goals of the council—activities, communication, and education—acing our family unity. We spent a whole weekend with family, all generations, with a variety of activities. We created lasting memories and made it fun and engaging—that was the magic, and it made all the difference.

These types of events became attraction-based and proved to be a natural way to bridge the generations. Making wine became a tradition and has been the centerpiece for our events, evolving over time to an annual weekend. Together we learned to demonstrate it, do it, and live it for our family to see the benefits of an organized family structure. This framework has strengthened our family, reconnected us to our roots, and preserved the culture of our founders. It is a work in progress and continues to grow.

In the beginning, my family did not understand the foreign concept of family governance. Today, the unfamiliar is familiar. It is natural for a family to grow—not only in size, also growing in needs. My driving philosophy has been, "Start where you are and grow as you go." Like the law of the farm, it is a slow process, things take time, and patience is key. Good things come to those who wait, and even greater things come to those who wait longer—much longer.

There are many examples of families and businesses not making it past the third generation. We continue to be a strong business and strong family. With G3 firmly at the helm and G4 and G5 paving their way, our story continues...

SEVEN

It's a Relay, Not a Sprint

For us, the process of implementing family governance started slowly and has progressed over the past fifteen years. We have come a long way and we have a long way to go. As Ernest often said about growing the business, "We are just scratching the surface."

It reminds me of one of my favorite Aesop's fables, where the moral of the story is—slow and steady wins the race.

The Tortoise and the Hare

A hare was one day making fun of a tortoise for being so slow upon his feet. "Wait a bit," said the tortoise. "I'll run a race with you, and I'll wager that I'll win."

"Oh well," replied the hare, who was much amused at the idea, "let's try and see." And it was soon agreed that the fox should set a course for them and be the judge. When the time came, both started off together, but the hare was soon so far ahead that he thought he might as well have a rest. So down he lay and fell fast asleep.

Meanwhile the tortoise kept plodding on, and in time reached the goal. At last the hare woke up with a start and dashed on at his fastest, but only to find that the tortoise had already won the race."

—*Aesop's Fables*

As a child I loved reading Aesop's Fables. I related to the cleverness of the stories and morals subtly communicated, offering words of wisdom in the form of lessons that can be applied in everyday life. In this story of the tortoise and the hare, I take the analogy further to describe multi-generational families and their longevity over time—it is a relay, not a sprint. One person can take the lead, though it takes many to win the race, especially over time and with each succeeding generation.

There is no fast track when it comes to family, especially given that there are many people, personalities, generations, branches, and geographic locations. Do you want to get there faster? Where is "there?" In families, that is a good question. Getting "there" creates more questions than answers. In this extraordinary time, the world has slowed down long enough for us to catch our breath, get clear, and put one foot in front of the other, knowing it is not about getting "there," it is about getting in the "race."

There is no cookie cutter solution when it comes to forming a family governance mindset or culture alongside the business, it is an integrated approach. It is a process to make your own. I became the catalyst, stepped up, and took action in my family. We made a lot of progress, creating a foundation of structure, systems, and processes before they were needed. Now what? How would we make it sustainable? A proactive plan was needed to grow from "me" to "we."

From Me to We

Early on I was doing a lot on my own—creating a structure for family governance, activities, communication, and education. It was consuming a lot of time and not all family members were onboard. I persevered and kept focused on things that mattered and were in my sphere of influence. The council added more activities and structure. With each passing year, other family members stepped up on specific projects and programs, helping out when available.

While continuing to grow organically and creating more activities, the need for dedicated committees was essential. Originally, we did not have committees—they were slowly added based on need and interest. We have evolved through trial and error and adapted to reflect the current needs of today. I could see new committee members getting frustrated, and would say, "Welcome to my world!" I was enthused by their concern and interest to improve the process. They frequently asked, "Why can't we do this faster and more efficiently?" or "Why aren't more people showing up?" and I would answer, "Those are the same

questions I asked myself many times in the beginning."
When we first started, things were slow—very slow. I did
not get frustrated, I remained patient and knew answers
would be revealed in time. It is all about time and timing,
we were ready for certain things and not for others, at
least not yet. Now we have four committees—Events,
Communication, Education, and NexGen.

We also needed solid support to maintain and grow. I
implemented a plan to professionalize the process with
dedicated staff to support our initiatives. This allowed the
council to be more strategically focused.

For long-term sustainability, I needed a partner. While
I knew family governance, I needed a co-chair, ideally
someone working in the business, representing another
branch of our family and based in Modesto. I immediately
thought of my cousin Stephanie. She was Vice President
of Marketing at the time, and is now CMO. The sentiment
from other council members was "Good luck with that,
she's too busy." I contacted her, presented my vision,
and persuaded her to join me as co-chair. This provided
balance—she works in the business, is located in Modesto,
and is from Ernest's side of the family, while I am from
Julio's side. We also have complementary skill sets, making
it a strong partnership. This framework established a model

for future generations by creating a range of opportunities to participate, from leading committees to just showing up at events.

I learned to have zero expectations, recognizing that family members have differing levels of bandwidth at different stages of life. Instead, when it comes to engagement, my mantra is "Work with the willing." That is, appeal to family members who are responsive and positive, celebrating those who could attend and continuing to invite those who could not, while not making them feel guilty for not being there. Being inclusive versus exclusive made all the difference to increasing participation.

At certain stages, some in our family may have thought things were going too fast, some may have thought too slow, and some may have thought just right. That is how it is in a family—it is impossible to please everyone all the time, so it is best to look for how you can please most of the people most of the time.

Going to the "fun side" not only increased engagement, it also alleviated tension. When fermenting wine in small barrels, carbon dioxide builds up pressure within the barrel. If not released, it can explode. The barrel bung, acting as a release valve, is designed to allow just enough pressure for fermentation to continue in the barrel and the excess to be released as needed.

It is the same way in families. Unless there is a "release valve," pressure and resentment can build over time. By creating a proactive outlet with meaningful roles, it provides opportunity for engagement for all family members, whether they work in the business or not.

I often got asked in the beginning, especially when there was little attendance or they would see me working very hard, "Why are you doing this?" My first response was, "Because it's the right thing to do." I feel the same today.

I learned along the way that not everyone likes change. It can be scary, especially if you have a set way of doing things. For families it can be even more so, especially if a certain way is "the way." For this reason, change can be a challenge to grasp—it can be viewed as risky, or even fearful. For example, while the younger generation often pushes for change, the older generation may prefer the status quo and wants to keep things the way they are. Resistance to change is natural. Not everyone sees the same vision at first, and it takes time to recognize the benefits and rewards.

Gamechangers

There are many contributing factors to effectively navigate the three-circle model. Some happen quickly, and some stand the test of time. Some are very tactical, and some are more philosophical. Some are gamechangers. What is a *gamechanger*? It is a newly introduced element that changes an existing situation or activity in a significant way. What were the gamechangers for our family? There were three of significance.

The first was becoming the catalyst, a self-imposed leader, and taking action. It solidified the power of one, where one person can make a difference. It allowed me to start with my own generation and build from there. The greatest compliment I received from my family was, "If you did not step up, we would not be doing this today."

The second gamechanger was knowing my family and what worked best for us. I knew I needed metrics to introduce and "sell" the idea of family governance. By sharing industry best practices and data anonymously collected from the assessment, I made an informed recommendation to my family. Unanimous consensus was reached, and we started our family council.

The third gamechanger was taking the tension out and making things fun. We created activities that were inclusive and attraction-based, increasing excitement and engagement across generations. We re-created family traditions in a new and different way in locations conducive for promoting interaction and communication.

I have concluded it is about managing the dynamics of the three-circle model. No matter who the cast of characters are in the family, there is a role—for everyone. Everyone can be involved, whether it is to create something large and impactful or something small and meaningful. The process requires planning, patience, and commitment for the long haul—it is a relay, not a sprint.

Evolution to Premier Growth

During this process, I combined my professional and personal expertise with my passion for bridging the gap between business and family, and I founded my business in 2010. During this time, I realized I could help other families help themselves in similar ways. It seemed like the natural next step to explore, sparking my entrepreneurial spirt. Others might find cumbersome the things I find exciting and excel at—like bringing family together physically or virtually, inviting impact by gaining perspectives from all family members through proactive planning, mentoring, and collaborating. I never thought I could do what I love and make a business out of it. It goes back to the advice I got early on, "Find something you love to do, and you'll never work a day in your life." Wise words.

Premier Growth is in the business of family, empowering families with modern-day solutions to cultivate thriving legacies. I mentor individuals, advocate for families, and collaborate with professionals to help navigate a path to professionalizing the family while personalizing the business. My greatest reward has been to take the business skills I learned and apply them to the family, in what I call professionalizing the family. I also learned the importance of creating a long-term plan, one that is not exclusively financial, and focuses on the value of the family as the wealth creator of legacy, which is what I call personalizing the business.

The name *Premier Growth* stems from two of the most famous wine regions in the world—Burgundy and Bordeaux. Burgundy is renowned for Premier Cru, and Bordeaux is renowned for First Growth wines. Those who are familiar with these regions know that you would never think of combining them. By merging these terms, it represented my way of blending traditional and modern-day ideas, offering a new perspective in the world of family business.

"The Business of Family" is rooted in the large family I was born into. As long as I can remember, there was lots and lots of activity all around. The need for order, discipline, routine, and purpose became hallmarks of our family. Watching and learning as my parents managed eight children, teaching us that family comes first, I was gaining the most valuable gifts in life, ones that I am now sharing with others.

My Next Mountain

My dad played a big part in my personal growth journey when I was growing up. At different stages he introduced age-appropriate knowledge on business and personal growth topics. He has always been proactive in forwarding books and articles to me, my siblings, and his grandchildren on various subjects including business, leadership, and spirituality.

Last year, he gave me a book titled *The Second Mountain* by David Brooks. It caught my eye since I had just returned from Bhutan. I related well to this book as it describes the differences between climbing the first and second mountains in life. The first mountain is defined by our culture today as achieving individual success, making your mark, and experiencing personal happiness. The second mountain that Brooks describes is moving from self-centered to other-centered, seeking higher meaning. This describes my journey.

In Bhutan, I had a chance to see some of the highest mountains in the world and I climbed some and admired many from afar, imagining what it would be like to climb to that level of elevation. I was seeking a higher place and greater purpose. With baby steps, the elevation or place we think is too high becomes surmountable. Yes, there will be bumps to endure, mountains to climb, valleys and rivers to cross—however, staying true to ourselves and our purpose provides an anchor of strength to navigate the rough seas ahead.

Our world has changed, and it is challenging us. Now more than ever, having solid roots is what will allow us to thrive and make it through all of what we are facing. I feel it is time we honor each moment and focus on what is most important—the people, places, and things in our lives that matter, starting with ourselves, our family, and the legacy we want to build for the future.

EIGHT

Creating Our Future

Hope is being able to see that there is light despite all of the darkness.

—*Desmond Tutu*

As 2020 approached, I was expecting a monumental year. It started out very hopeful and I had many plans. Then it suddenly took an unexpected turn, filled with fear, disappointment, controversy, confusion, and no clear idea of what the future would hold. Staying positive in the unknown has been a challenge.

In this "great pause," I have seen drastic change in our world, from moving at a frenetic pace to a near-total global shutdown. We were forced to make a paradigm shift in the way we live and look forward. Slowing down and considering all that is going on around us has become paramount. We have yet to know exactly how these dynamics will impact our lives in the long run.

For me, it has been a culminating year in many ways. I have learned to take better care of my health and well-being, and to slow down, appreciating the absence of chaos and busyness that used to fill my days. I have taken time to get back to basics, and rediscover what is important. I have felt a significant shift inside of me, like the phoenix rising from the ashes, the ultimate cleansing of the past, and to adopt and allow a new approach to life. Even though the future is unknown, I see light ahead.

Hindsight is 2020

Do the best you can until you know better. Then when you know better, do better.

—*Maya Angelo*

In this extraordinary year I have realized that hindsight is indeed 2020. As I reflect on my life experiences and the choices I made in the past that seemed difficult, blurred by chaos and confusion at the time, I now see them clearly after knowing the outcome.

What has crystalized for me is that knowledge is the understanding we gain through study or experience and wisdom is the ability to discern or judge what is true, right, or lasting. Wisdom is revealed by what a person does, not by what they know.

Having swirled all of my life knowledge, experience, and expertise together, there are things I know now and wish I knew then. I realize the point of life is not about coming out unscathed and perfect. It is about finding our own way, right or wrong, good or bad, to make mistakes, get messy and cross our fingers, and that we come out alive to talk about it.

Even though it is impossible to distill every lesson, anecdote, or pearl of wisdom I gained, there is one core gem of personal insight that was significant for me—it was learning to be self-aware.

Since most of my life was spent in unconscious chaos and always being on the go, I took little time out for my own self-awareness. By turning the mirror around and reflecting on all aspects of myself, I am able to see who I really am with compassion and authenticity. In the past, it was challenging for me to define my own feelings, emotions, and desires. Now, when I listen to myself, and what the universe is trying to "tell" me, it is quite inspiring and enlightening. Being self-aware provides a lens through which to make purposeful choices and positive change. Introspection is imperative to self-awareness, and in my case, I needed to dig deep to see clearly.

By being self-aware, I am able to respectfully and compassionately take responsibility for my own actions, without fear or judgement. With each step forward, with each difficult choice I made in life, I was learning to lean into my own destiny. I had many role models who gave me a solid foundation from which to grow and thrive. It is clear to me that no-one was holding me back except myself.

I know now that we are *all* meant to shine.

> "*Our deepest fear is not that we are inadequate. Our deepest fear is that we are powerful beyond measure. It is our light, not our darkness that most frightens us. We ask ourselves, 'Who am I to be brilliant, gorgeous, talented, fabulous?' Actually, who are you not to be? You are a child of God. Your playing small does not serve the world. There is nothing enlightened about shrinking so that other people won't feel insecure around you. We are all meant to shine, as children do. We were born to make manifest the glory of God that is within us. It's not just in some of us; it's in everyone. And as we let our own light shine, we unconsciously give other people permission to do the same. As we are liberated from our own fear, our presence automatically liberates others.*"

> —*Marianne Williamson, A Return to Love: Reflections on the Principles of A Course in Miracles, 1992*

From Fear to Foresight

Telling the story of my journey has been a cathartic experience, transporting me from a place of fear to foresight, to what I know now and wish to carry forward. Looking back allows us to honor our past, acknowledge the lessons learned, and choose what to carry into the future. Writing this book forced me to step outside my comfort zone and face the fear of revealing myself. I learned I had to get out of my own way and not dim my light.

By facing my fear and bringing my vision to reality with the completion of this book, I have taken a quantum leap, revealing my vulnerabilities in an authentic and empowering way.

To know thyself is the beginning of wisdom.

—Socrates

When I was young, I had no appreciation for Socrates's maxim "Know thyself." I thought I knew exactly who I was—after all, I have had years of experience with myself. I came to realize that my identity had been closely tied to my family and working in the business. At first, it was difficult to understand who I was beyond the shade of the family tree. Once I knew myself better, I knew how I could best contribute to my family and to the world.

This concept of *Self, Family, World* is one that I created and now use in my professional work. I outline these three key areas to help guide others who may be discovering their own way, whether it is inside or outside the shade of the family tree.

Self—Embrace Your Own Power

By knowing yourself and stepping into your own power, you can see how to best contribute to your family. It is our individual strength that allows us to move forward in our lives, creating our own stories, while still remaining connected to the family.

Family—Stay True to Your Roots

Family values provide the foundation from which to grow. Your values along with common goals and purpose help foster family unity across generations. By honoring and living your family culture, there is greater opportunity to flourish and evolve over time.

World—Be a Better Global Citizen

When you know yourself and are guided by strong family values, you are better able to show up and engage in the world. By being informed and educated, you can participate actively as an individual or together as a family and contribute to the world in a way that matters most to you.

Children Learn What They Live

If children live with criticism, they learn to condemn.
If children live with hostility, they learn to fight.
If children live with fear, they learn to be
*   apprehensive.*
If children live with pity, they learn to feel sorry for
*   themselves.*
If children live with ridicule, they learn to feel shy.
If children live with jealousy, they learn to feel envy.
If children live with shame, they learn to feel guilty.
If children live with encouragement, they learn
*   confidence.*
If children live with tolerance, they learn patience.
If children live with praise, they learn appreciation.
If children live with acceptance, they learn to love.
If children live with approval, they learn to like
*   themselves.*
If children live with recognition, they learn it is good to
*   have a goal.*
If children live with sharing, they learn generosity.
If children live with honesty, they learn truthfulness.

If children live with fairness, they learn justice.
If children live with kindness and consideration, they
  learn respect.
If children live with security, they learn to have faith
  in themselves and in those about them.
If children live with friendliness, they learn the world
  is a nice place in which to live.

—*Dorothy Law Nolte, 1972*

I remember this poem hanging on a wall in our home growing up and it always had a profound effect on me. The message is clear—children learn from the way they live. I was shaped by my family's values, the way we lived, and our love for one another. It was the glue holding us together. Our bond as a family was our togetherness, staying connected in everyday moments, celebrations, holidays, and going to church as a family. They are my roots and through them I learned how to walk through the world.

In our modern era of technology, social media, and globalization, the role of family is heightened. We have become accustomed to fast and immediate gratification in our complicated and speedy culture. With mixed messages creating division and confusion, the importance of being a good role model is critical. The future of our world will continue to change in ways that we cannot even imagine, affecting how we interact socially, professionally, and with our families.

It is time to embrace change and growth, allowing our values to guide us through unfamiliar territory.

The next generation is unknowingly preparing themselves for the future, with a mindset far different from our own. Fostering their growth, listening to their perspectives, and staying connected, no matter where their life takes them, is the best thing we can do to create a thriving future for our children.

Dorothy Law Nolte also published a book in 1998 called *Children Learn What They Live—Parenting to Inspire Values,* and it became a cornerstone for parenting my own children. Even though her book was written twenty-two years ago, and her poem was written forty-eight years ago, their sentiment rings true now more than ever. It is our children who will live with the decisions and actions we take now. The closing excerpt of her book perfectly captures this notion.

Linking the Past with the Future

The general tone of our everyday lives together will affect our children's memories of our family life. These experiences and relationships will go with them into their relationships, their marriages, their own families, and their futures as a whole.

As I've said so many times, it is what we do with our children that counts, much more than we say or even what we believe. Our values are transmitted across the generations through our behavior. Our children witness and absorb the way we live together day-to-day, and what they learn serves as a model for them all their lives, affecting not only them, but their children. We think of our loving actions as a kind of chain of love that stretches both forward and back across generations.

Giving our children a world filled with encouragement, tolerance, and praise; a world in which they receive our acceptance, approval, and recognition; a world where they can share honestly and expect fairness, kindness, and consideration in return, can make a real difference in their lives and in the quality of life for everyone around them.

Let's expect the best of our children – and in fact, of all children: the kids down the street, the kids across town, kids far away. Let's do all we can to make it easy for them to do their best. After all, it's our neighborhood, our town, our country, our planet. Let's do what we can to ensure that our children will be part of a future that gradually eliminates fear, hunger, prejudice, and intolerance—a future that includes the acceptance of every person on our planet into the family of mankind.

Let's pave the way for children to see the world in the best light, so that they'll find it – and can help make it—a nice place to live.

The path behind me and the path ahead of me look quite different. My story has been a discovery process, not all revealed at once. Every turn, every decision, every choice I have made, from growing up to surviving a near-death experience, have culminated to where I am today. I feel as if I have climbed my third mountain and beyond.

Writing this book has been a significant life-changer for me. It is a highlight of my personal and professional life that have been intertwined. I have been sculpted by people, places, and experiences along my life journey. I treasure those who influenced my life adventure and am grateful to them all—past, present, and future.

As I reflect on my life and the major events transpiring during this pivotal year, I look forward to what lies ahead with optimism and hope. Now with greater purpose and being rooted in family, I honor my past and the choices I made, I take the lessons I learned and the wisdom I gained to move forward and contribute to creating a thriving future for generations to come.

Passing the torch to the next generation—
Alexandra, Coleman, Allison, and Cameron

REFERENCES

Books

Aesop's Fables

Brooks, David—*The Second Mountain*, 2019

Campbell, Joseph—*The Hero with a Thousand Faces*, 1949

Chatwin, Bruce—*The Songlines*, 1987

Coleman, Alfred—*Sticks—A Story of Triumph Over Disability*, 2004

Dickens, Charles—*A Tale of Two Cities*, 1859

Gladwell, Malcolm—*The Tipping Point*, 2000

Henderson, Bruce with Gallo, Ernest and Gallo, Julio—*Ernest & Julio: Our Story*, 1994

Murdock, Maureen—*The Heroine's Journey*, 1990

Nolte, Dorothy Law—*Children Learn What They Live: Parenting to Inspire Values,* 1998

Suess, Dr.—*Oh, the You'll Places you Will Go!* 1990

Resource

FEAT—Family Enterprise Assessment Tool
www.premiergrowth.com/feat

ABOUT THE AUTHOR

Caroline Coleman Bailey is a seasoned expert in The Business of Family. As a third-generation member of the Gallo family, and following an eighteen-year career in the family business, Caroline pursued her own entrepreneurial spirit. Through this transition, she identified her value within the family as a catalyst, launching the Gallo Family Council in 2006, as the founding chair.

Caroline understands the dynamics of multi-generational families. She is one of eight children and a mother of four. She is a daughter, granddaughter, sister, aunt, and cousin. In these complex times, she saw a need to create modern day solutions to encourage family unity and cultivate connections for like-minded individuals and families in business together.

Combining her professional and personal expertise with her passion for bridging the gap between business and family, Caroline founded Premier Growth® in 2010. She works with individuals, families, and professionals to navigate a path of unity by professionalizing the family while personalizing the business.

For more information please visit www.premiergrowth.com

ACKNOWLEDGEMENTS

I am grateful to all those who made my vision a reality.

To Stacey Conrad, who was by my side every step along the way and has known me and my family since working in our family business. Your motivation kept me strong and focused throughout. Your professionalism and dedication are supreme.

To Jennifer Kimpe of Bien Sur, who provided strategic input and guidance while staying positive and supportive throughout this unexpected project.

To Sophia Mavrides of Sophia Studio, who worked her magic on interior photos and provided inspiration for my book cover design.

To Mark Leonard, my publishing partner, who guided the process and provided direction on content, flow and execution. I appreciate your expertise, patience, and flexibility as I transitioned from the original intent of this book.

To all those who provided praise for my book, I am grateful you stepped up so quickly to write such kind and thoughtful words. I am pleased my story resonated with each of you.

To my dear friends, my high school girlfriends who get me no matter what, my global goddesses who have taken me places, my local community friendships who are always there in time of need, and my world of friendships gained on my personal and professional path. Your presence in my life has been the greatest gift. I am thankful for your friendship.

To my dearest D, thank you for unknowingly reminding me of the true meaning of authenticity, vulnerability, and unconditional love. You have been a guiding light and inspiration. I am truly grateful to you, forever and a day.

To my children—Alexandra, Coleman, Allison, and Cameron—for your love and patience with me as I found my way. You have been my greatest teachers, challenging me at every turn. I hope you find meaning in my words and inspiration in my actions to discover your own way in life. May you find joy and satisfaction in all you do.

To my siblings—Chris, Greg, Brad, Joan, Ted, Tim, and Anne—for your passion and perseverance in all you aim to be and do in this world. Despite all the bumps and bruises, I am thankful to be your sister. I cherish the memorable moments we have shared and look forward to many more to come. I am proud of our unity.

To my parents for their love, guidance, and encouragement lavished upon me throughout my life. Your presence, not only in my life, also in my children's lives will always be remembered. Thank you for your wisdom, tenacity, and dedicated faith in making our family and our world a better place for generations to come.

To my grandparents and relatives who have passed before me, for your humble beginnings that paved the way for me and my family. I honor your time, talent, and treasure always. I am in the shade today because you planted a tree long ago.

To my extended family, current and future, here's to us as we unite together for generations to come—our story continues...

IN MEMORIAM

I would like to pay tribute to two special people who passed away in 2020.

The Captain, Bill Bowers

Founder of Captain's Tavern Restaurant
June 28, 1929—September 17, 2020

The Captain in his restaurant in Miami, Florida

Thank you, Captain, for your infectious spirit and your contribution to our annual harvest stone crab lunch. You left a lasting impression on all of us who celebrated under Julio's tree and beyond. We cherish the memories of this treasured tradition.

Jamie Redford
Co-Founder of Redford Center and KPJR Films
May 5, 1962- October 16, 2020

*Jamie Redford and me at MacMurray Ranch
in Sonoma County, 2017*

Thank you, Jamie, for being a special guest at one of my
Premier Growth events and sharing your own story with
me. You were a fierce advocate for the power of storytelling
and inspired me and many others to do the same. Your light
will continue to shine bright in our world.

POSTSCRIPT

During the writing of this book, and as I was gathering pieces of our family history, I came across this postscript from the book *Ernest & Julio—Our Story*. When I read it, I was moved for many reasons and felt compelled to share it with you. It is remarkable how relevant the message still is today, a message of hope and achievement against all odds and is inspiring for future generations.

Ernest

Fortune has a way of favoring those in the right place at the right time, which is exactly where Julio and I were as young men in 1933.

We could easily have been discouraged by what we had heard from our elders and never started our winery. In hindsight, it would appear that we had no reasonable chance of surviving. The odds against us were formidable when we set out on our course. The country was in the depth of the Great Depression, and we were facing comparatively large, established, well-financed (and often government-financed) competitors. We didn't even know how to make wine commercially when we decided to start our winery. We were challenged by the hardships of our youth, by the Depression, and by the loss of our parents.

By nature we were never satisfied with doing anything less than well. Each of us was guided by one principle: to strive for perfection. We never achieved perfection, but we constantly kept trying.

We both knew when we started that we had to make quality products and sell them at fair and competitive prices if we were to succeed. We believed then, and now, that there is an overriding imperative that private enterprise must provide real value to the consumer if it is to be rewarded with a legitimate, long-range profit.

When we introduced our varietal wines, there were no products better and few as good. We feel that this remains true today, when we make wines at every price level up to sixty dollars a bottle. We have given American wine consumers the greatest value— outstanding quality at reasonable prices—in every category in which we do business, and the consumers have responded accordingly.

From the beginning, Julio and I have been fortunate in finding employees and distributors who believe, as we do, that striving for perfection is a way of life.

With perfection as our goal, we have always tried to do our best—grape-growing, winemaking, production, marketing, salesmanship. It is still a goal for which we continue to strive in every aspect of our business.

Along with our colleagues in the wine business, we helped transform the small struggling industry we entered in 1933 into a consumer-responsive national and international business of world-class stature, and the best is yet to come. The wine industry has some great things going for it as we look to the twenty-first century:

- The weight of medical and scientific evidence regarding the health benefits of responsible wine consumption, from such prestigious medical schools as Harvard and the University of California (Davis), among others, is expanding to the point of irrefutability. As the consumer becomes increasingly aware of the unquestionable benefits of wine, consumption of wine will increase to the benefit of all.

- The program we initiated some years ago of long-term contracts to encourage growers to replant their vineyards with fine varietal grapes has significantly contributed to the great improvement of the types of grapes now available in California for the production of world-class wines.

- Advancing enological research and technology is resulting in new and better products.

After having lived a lifetime in the wine business, we continue to see infinite possibilities.

We feel that our industry provides and will continue to provide people with one of the greatest things in life—an enjoyable beverage with strong familial, communal, cultural, and even religious ties.

We wrote of our experiences in the hope that our story might serve as encouragement to others—particularly the young—that our country's system works for those with the commitment to succeed. There is a great need to preserve our system of free enterprise under which this was all possible.

A final note

I hope our story will be inspiring, particularly to the young, that if they have the will to work hard and make a strong commitment to succeed, the American system works for everyone. Not only for people of wealth, but also for sons of immigrants who have nothing.

—*Julio R. Gallo*

POSTSCRIPT

My brother Julio died on May 2, 1993, in a jeep accident on his son's ranch west of Modesto. He was eighty-three.

Julio was a great brother, a great partner, and a great human being. His passing is an enormous personal loss to me, and both of our families. There are no words to describe how much we miss him.

—Ernest Gallo

CPSIA information can be obtained
at www.ICGtesting.com
Printed in the USA
BVHW010617221220
595989BV00016B/20/J